Desserts

Bath · New York · Singapore · Hong Kong · Cologne · Delhi · Melbourne

This edition published by Parragon in 2009

Parragon Publishing
Queen Street House
4 Queen Street
Bath BA1 1HE, UK

Copyright © Parragon Books Ltd 2007
Internal Design by Terry Jeavons & Company

ISBN 978-1-4075-8028-9

Printed in China

Notes for the Reader
This book uses imperial, metric, and U.S. cup measurements. Follow the same units of measurement throughout; do not mix imperial and metric. All spoon measurements are level: teaspoons are assumed to be 5 ml, and tablespoons are assumed to be 15 ml. Unless otherwise stated, milk is assumed to be whole, eggs and individual vegetables, such as potatoes, are medium, and pepper is freshly ground black pepper.

The times given are an approximate guide only. Preparation times differ according to the techniques used by different people and the cooking times may also vary from those given as a result of the type of oven used. Optional ingredients, variations, or serving suggestions have not been included in the calculations.

Recipes using raw or very lightly cooked eggs should be avoided by infants, the elderly, pregnant women, convalescents, and anyone with a chronic condition. Pregnant and breastfeeding women are advised to avoid eating peanuts and peanut products. People with nut allergies should be aware that some of the prepared ingredients used in the recipes in this book may contain nuts. Always check the packaging before use.

Picture acknowledgements
The publisher would like to thank Duane Reider/Getty Images for permission to reproduce copyright material for the front cover

Desserts

introduction

No matter how filling, tasty, and satisfying your main dish is, there always seems to be just enough room left for dessert! If you are one of those people who cannot resist a sideways glance at the dessert trolley as it rolls past your table in your favorite restaurant, then this is the book for you.

A dessert is called upon to play many roles. Cookies and bars, for example, are not only a great way to round off a simple midweek lunch or supper dish, they also make perfect partners for morning coffee and afternoon tea, and are wonderful for late-night snacking. A batch of fragrant cookies or brownies, still warm and fresh from

the oven, seems to symbolize "home" and "comfort" more than any other food, and is marvelous for serving to neighbors who call in for dessert and a chat, or to take as a gift when you are visiting friends or family.

Pies and tarts in all their guises are incredibly versatile—they can be homely or sophisticated, traditional or modern, and are sometimes a little of both, a contemporary take on an old idea that produces a delicious result!

Fruit-based desserts are ideal if you are serving a filling main dish but still want something sweet to round off the meal. They are also a great way to make the most of those seasonal fruits, such as summer berries, that are only available for a few short but very special weeks each year.

Chilled desserts, ice creams, and refreshing sherbets are an elegant way to end a stylish dinner party at any time of year, and are an obvious choice for summer lunch parties, especially if you

are eating alfresco. And of course a rich, creamy, delectable ice cream has to be the ultimate comfort food—think of all those great movies where the unhappy heroine and her friends tuck into giant tubs of their favorite flavor! When it's homemade, it's even better!

cookies & bars

A melt-in-the-mouth, home-baked cookie or bar makes the perfect end to a meal. If you find chocolate irresistible, there are plenty of gorgeous recipes in this chapter so that you can indulge in an occasional treat. To serve with coffee on very special occasions, give in to Chocolate Temptations—but resist the temptation to eat the cookies before you've decorated them, because they really are even more attractive with their stripes of bittersweet and white chocolate. Cookie & Cream Sandwiches will also satisfy chocolate cravings—two cookies flavored with the merest hint of cinnamon and sandwiched with a chocolate-cream filling. Brownie-lovers are spoilt for choice with recipes for Double Chocolate Chip Brownies, White Chocolate Brownies, and Pecan Brownies, while children will enjoy eating Zebra Cookies, with zebra "markings" created by milk and white chocolate buttons. Caramel Chocolate Shortbread is often called "Millionaire's Shortbread"—try it, and you'll soon discover why. It's just divine!

For those occasions when something a little less rich is called for, try Oatmeal & Pecan Cookies or Oat & Hazelnut Morsels—absolutely delicious cookies baked to a crisp on the outside and with soft, chewy centers. Very satisfying!

chocolate temptations

ingredients

MAKES 24

12¹/₂ oz/350 g bittersweet
 chocolate

6 oz/175 g unsalted butter,
 plus extra for greasing

1 tsp strong coffee

2 eggs

4 oz/115 g/scant ³/₄ cup soft
 brown sugar

6 oz/175 g/scant 1¹/₄ cups
 all-purpose flour

¹/₄ tsp baking powder

pinch of salt

2 tsp almond extract

2 oz/55 g/generous ¹/₂ cup
 Brazil nuts, chopped

2 oz/55 g/generous ¹/₂ cup
 hazelnuts, chopped

1¹/₂ oz/40 g white chocolate

method

1 Place 8 oz/225 g of the bittersweet chocolate with the butter and coffee in a heatproof bowl set over a pan of gently simmering water and heat until the chocolate is almost melted.

2 Meanwhile, beat the eggs in a bowl until fluffy. Gradually whisk in the sugar until thick. Remove the chocolate from the heat and stir until smooth. Add to the egg mixture and stir until combined.

3 Sift the flour, baking powder, and salt into a bowl, then stir into the chocolate mixture. Chop 3 oz/85 g of the remaining bittersweet chocolate into pieces and stir into the mixture. Stir in the almond extract and chopped nuts.

4 Put 24 tablespoonfuls of the mixture onto 1 or 2 large, greased cookie sheets, then transfer to a preheated oven, 350°F/180°C, and bake for 16 minutes. Remove from the oven and transfer to a wire rack to cool. To decorate, melt the remaining chocolate (bittersweet and white) in turn as earlier, then spoon into a pastry bag and pipe thin lines onto the cookies.

pineapple & cherry florentines

ingredients

MAKES ABOUT 14

4 tbsp unsalted butter

$1^1/_2$ oz/40 g/scant $^1/_4$ cup raw brown sugar

1 tbsp corn syrup

$1^3/_4$ oz/50 g/generous $^1/_3$ cup all-purpose flour, sifted

1 oz/25 g/$^1/_8$ cup angelica, coarsely chopped

1 oz/25 g/$^1/_8$ cup candied cherries, coarsely chopped

2 oz/55 g/$^1/_2$ cup slivered almonds, coarsely chopped

2 oz/55 g/$^1/_3$ cup candied pineapple, coarsely chopped

1 tsp lemon juice

4 oz/115 g bittersweet chocolate, melted and cooled

method

1 Place the butter, sugar, and syrup in a pan and heat gently until melted, then stir in the flour, angelica, cherries, almonds, pineapple, and lemon juice.

2 Place walnut-size mounds of the mixture, spaced well apart, on 1 or 2 large cookie sheets lined with nonstick parchment paper and flatten gently with a fork. Bake in a preheated oven, 350°F/180°C, for 8–10 minutes, or until golden brown. Use a spatula to neaten the ragged edges. Let cool for 1 minute, then transfer to a wire rack to cool completely.

3 Spread the melted chocolate over the base of each florentine, then place chocolate-side up on a cooling rack. Use a fork to mark the chocolate with wavy lines. Let stand until set.

cookie & cream sandwiches

ingredients

MAKES 12

4^1/2 oz/130 g unsalted butter, softened

4^1/2 oz/130 g/^{3}/4 cup golden confectioners' sugar

4^1/2 oz/130 g/scant 1 cup all-purpose flour

2 oz/55 g/scant ^{1}/2 cup unsweetened cocoa

^{1}/2 tsp ground cinnamon

filling

4^1/2 oz/130 g bittersweet chocolate, broken into pieces

4 tbsp heavy cream

method

1 Place the butter and sugar in a large bowl and beat together until light and fluffy. Sift the flour, unsweetened cocoa, and ground cinnamon into the bowl and mix until a smooth dough forms.

2 Place the dough between 2 sheets of nonstick parchment paper and roll out to ^{1}/8 inch/3 mm thick. Stamp out 2^1/2-inch/ 6-cm circles and place on a cookie sheet lined with nonstick parchment paper. Bake in a preheated oven, 325°F/160°C, for 15 minutes, until firm to the touch. Let cool for 2 minutes, then transfer to wire racks to cool completely.

3 To make the filling, place the chocolate and cream in a pan and heat gently until the chocolate has melted. Stir until smooth. Let cool, then let chill in the refrigerator for 2 hours, or until firm. Sandwich the cookies together in pairs with a spoonful of chocolate cream and serve.

double chocolate chip cookies

ingredients

MAKES 24

4 oz/115 g unsalted butter,
softened, plus extra for
greasing

2 oz/55 g/generous $^1/_4$ cup
golden granulated sugar

2 oz/55 g/generous $^1/_4$ cup
light brown sugar

1 egg, beaten

$^1/_2$ tsp vanilla extract

4 oz/115 g/generous $^3/_4$ cup
all-purpose flour

2 tbsp unsweetened cocoa

$^1/_2$ tsp baking soda

4 oz/115 g/$^2/_3$ cup milk
chocolate chips

2 oz/55 g/$^1/_2$ cup walnuts,
coarsely chopped

method

1 Place the butter, granulated sugar, and light brown sugar in a bowl and beat until light and fluffy. Gradually beat in the egg and vanilla extract.

2 Sift the flour, cocoa, and baking soda into the mixture and stir in carefully. Stir in the chocolate chips and walnuts. Drop dessert-spoonfuls of the mixture onto 3 greased cookie sheets, spaced well apart to allow for spreading.

3 Bake in a preheated oven, 350°F/180°C, for 10–15 minutes, or until the mixture has spread and the cookies are beginning to feel firm. Remove from the oven and let cool on the cookie sheets for 2 minutes, before transferring to cooling racks.

chocolate chip cookies

ingredients

MAKES 20

4 oz/115 g unsalted butter, softened, plus extra for greasing

4 oz/115 g/generous $1/2$ cup light brown sugar

1 egg

4 oz/115 g/$2/3$ cup oatmeal

1 tbsp milk

1 tsp vanilla extract

$4^1/2$ oz/130 g/scant 1 cup all-purpose flour

1 tbsp unsweetened cocoa

$1/2$ tsp baking powder

6 oz/175 g bittersweet chocolate, broken into pieces

6 oz/175 g milk chocolate, broken into pieces

method

1 Place the butter and sugar in a bowl and beat together with a wooden spoon until light and fluffy.

2 Beat in the egg, then add the oatmeal, milk, and vanilla. Beat together until well blended. Sift the flour, cocoa, and baking powder into the mixture and stir. Stir in the chocolate pieces.

3 Place dessertspoonfuls of the mixture on 2 large, greased cookie sheets and flatten slightly with a fork. Bake in a preheated oven, 350°F/180°C, for 15 minutes, or until slightly risen and firm. Remove from the oven and cool on the cookie sheets for 2 minutes, then transfer to wire racks to cool completely.

oatmeal & pecan cookies

ingredients

MAKES 15

4 oz/115 g unsalted butter,
  softened, plus extra for
  greasing
3 oz/85 g/scant $^1/_2$ cup light
  brown sugar
1 egg, beaten
1$^1/_2$ oz/40 g/$^1/_3$ cup pecans,
  chopped
3 oz/85 g/generous $^1/_2$ cup
  all-purpose flour
$^1/_2$ tsp baking powder
2 oz/55 g/$^1/_3$ cup oatmeal

method

1 Place the butter and sugar in a bowl and beat until light and fluffy. Gradually beat in the egg, then stir in the nuts.

2 Sift the flour and baking powder into the mixture and add the oatmeal. Stir together until well combined. Drop dessertspoonfuls of the mixture onto 2 greased cookie sheets, spaced well apart to allow for spreading.

3 Bake in a preheated oven, 350°F/180°C, for 15 minutes, or until pale golden. Remove from the oven and let cool on the cookie sheets for 2 minutes, then transfer to wire racks to cool completely.

oat & hazelnut morsels

ingredients

MAKES 30

3 oz/85 g unsalted butter or margarine, plus extra for greasing

8 oz/225 g/scant 1¼ cups raw brown sugar

1 egg, beaten

4 tbsp milk

1 tsp vanilla extract

½ tsp almond extract

3 oz/85 g/generous ⅔ cup hazelnuts

5 oz/150 g/1 cup all-purpose flour

1½ tsp ground allspice

¼ tsp baking soda

pinch of salt

12 oz/350 g/2 cups oatmeal

3 oz/85 g/scant 1 cup golden raisins

method

1 Beat the butter and sugar together in a mixing bowl. Blend in the egg, milk, and vanilla and almond extracts until thoroughly combined. Chop the hazelnuts finely.

2 In a mixing bowl, sift the flour, allspice, baking soda, and salt together. Add to the creamed mixture slowly, stirring constantly. Mix in the oatmeal, golden raisins, and hazelnuts.

3 Put 30 rounded tablespoonfuls of the mixture onto 2 large, greased cookie sheets, spaced well apart to allow for spreading. Transfer to a preheated oven, 375°F/190°C, and bake for 12–15 minutes, or until the cookies are golden brown.

4 Remove the cookies from the oven and place on a wire rack to cool before serving.

hazelnut chocolate crunch

ingredients

MAKES 12

7 oz/200 g/generous 2 cups
   rolled oats
1¹/₂ oz/40 g/¹/₃ cup
   hazelnuts, lightly toasted
   and chopped
1³/₄ oz/50 g/generous ¹/₃ cup
   all-purpose flour
4 oz/115 g unsalted butter,
   plus extra for greasing
3 oz/85 g/scant ¹/₂ cup light
   brown sugar
2 tbsp corn syrup
2 oz/55 g/¹/₃ cup bittersweet
   chocolate chips

method

1 Mix the oats, nuts, and flour in a large bowl.

2 Place the butter, sugar, and syrup in a large pan and heat gently until the sugar has dissolved. Pour in the dry ingredients and mix well. Stir in the chocolate chips.

3 Turn the mixture into a greased 9-inch/ 23-cm shallow, square baking pan and bake in a preheated oven, 350°F/180°C, for 20–25 minutes, or until golden brown and firm to the touch. Using a knife, mark into 12 rectangles and let cool in the pan. Cut the hazelnut chocolate crunch bars with a sharp knife before carefully removing them from the pan.

zebra cookies

ingredients

MAKES 18–20

2 oz/55 g bittersweet
  chocolate, broken into
  pieces
5 oz/150 g/1 cup all-purpose
  flour
1 tsp baking powder
1 egg
5 oz/150 g/scant ³/₄ cup
  superfine sugar
4 tbsp corn oil, plus extra
  for oiling
¹/₂ tsp vanilla extract
2 tbsp confectioners' sugar
1 small package milk
  chocolate buttons (about
  30 buttons)
1 small package white
  chocolate buttons (about
  30 buttons)

method

1 Melt the bittersweet chocolate in a heatproof bowl set over a pan of gently simmering water. Remove from the heat and let cool. Sift the flour and baking powder together.

2 Meanwhile, in a large bowl, whisk the egg, sugar, oil, and vanilla extract together. Whisk in the cooled, melted chocolate until well blended, then gradually stir in the flour. Cover the bowl with plastic wrap and chill in the refrigerator for at least 3 hours.

3 Shape tablespoonfuls of the mixture into log shapes using your hands, each measuring about 2 inches/5 cm. Roll the logs generously in the confectioners' sugar, then place on 1–2 large, oiled cookie sheets, allowing room for the cookies to spread during cooking.

4 Bake the cookies in a preheated oven, 375°F/190°C, for 15 minutes, or until firm. Remove from the oven, and place 3 chocolate buttons down the center of each, alternating the colors. Transfer to a wire rack and let cool.

chocolate & coffee wholewheat cookies

ingredients

MAKES 24

3 oz/85 g unsalted butter or
   margarine, plus extra for
   greasing
8 oz/225 g/1 cup soft brown
   sugar
1 egg
2¹/₂ oz/70 g/¹/₂ cup
   all-purpose flour
1 tsp baking soda
pinch of salt
2 oz/55 g/scant ¹/₂ cup
   wholewheat flour
1 tbsp bran
8 oz/225 g/1¹/₃ cups
   semisweet chocolate chips
7 oz/200 g/generous 2 cups
   rolled oats
1 tbsp strong coffee
3 oz/85 g/²/₃ cup hazelnuts,
   toasted and chopped
   coarsely

method

1 Beat the butter and sugar together in a bowl.
Add the egg and beat well, using a hand
whisk if preferred.

2 In a separate bowl, sift together the all-
purpose flour, baking soda, and salt, then add
in the wholewheat flour and bran. Mix in the
egg mixture, then stir in the chocolate chips,
oats, coffee, and hazelnuts. Mix well, with an
electric whisk if preferred.

3 Put 24 rounded tablespoonfuls of the
mixture onto 2 large, greased cookie sheets,
leaving room for the cookies to spread during
cooking. Alternatively, with lightly floured
hands, break off pieces of the mixture and roll
into balls (about 1 oz/25 g each), then place
on the cookie sheets and flatten them with the
back of a teaspoon. Transfer the cookie sheets
to a preheated oven, 375°F/190°C, and bake
for 16–18 minutes, or until the cookies are
golden brown.

4 Remove from the oven, then transfer to a
cooling rack and let cool before serving.

mocha walnut cookies

ingredients

MAKES ABOUT 16

4 oz/115 g unsalted butter, softened, plus extra for greasing

4 oz/115 g/generous $^1/_2$ cup light brown sugar

4 oz/115 g/scant $^1/_2$ cup golden granulated sugar

1 tsp vanilla extract

1 tbsp instant coffee granules, dissolved in 1 tbsp hot water

1 egg

6 oz/175 g/scant 1$^1/_4$ cups all-purpose flour

$^1/_2$ tsp baking powder

$^1/_4$ tsp baking soda

2 oz/55 g/$^1/_3$ cup milk chocolate chips

2 oz/85 g/$^1/_2$ cup shelled walnuts, coarsely chopped

method

1 Place the butter, light brown sugar, and granulated sugar in a large bowl and beat together thoroughly until light and fluffy. Place the vanilla extract, coffee, and egg in a separate large bowl and whisk together.

2 Gradually add the coffee mixture to the butter and sugar, beating until fluffy. Sift the flour, baking powder, and baking soda into the mixture and fold in carefully. Fold in the chocolate chips and walnuts.

3 Drop dessertspoonfuls of the mixture onto 2 large cookie sheets, spacing well apart to allow room for spreading. Bake in a preheated oven, 350°F/180°C, for 10–15 minutes, or until crisp on the outside but still soft inside. Remove from the oven. Cool on the cookie sheets for 2 minutes, then transfer to wire racks to cool completely.

nutty drizzles

ingredients

MAKES 12

7 oz/200 g unsalted butter,
   plus extra for greasing
9 oz/250 g/generous 1¼ cups
   raw brown sugar
1 egg
4½ oz/130 g/scant 1 cup
   all-purpose flour, sifted
1 tsp baking powder
1 tsp baking soda
6 oz/175 g/1 cup oatmeal
1 tbsp bran
1 tbsp wheatgerm
4 oz/115 g mixed nuts,
   toasted and coarsely
   chopped
7 oz/200 g/generous 1 cup
   bittersweet chocolate
   chips
3 oz/85 g/scant 1 cup raisins
   and golden raisins
6 oz/175 g semisweet
   chocolate, coarsely
   chopped

method

1 In a large bowl, beat together the butter, sugar, and egg. Add the flour, baking powder, baking soda, oatmeal, bran, and wheatgerm and mix together until well combined. Stir in the nuts, chocolate chips, and dried fruit.

2 Put 24 rounded tablespoonfuls of the mixture onto 2 large, greased cookie sheets. Transfer to a preheated oven, 350°F/180°C, and bake for 12 minutes, or until the cookies are golden.

3 Remove the cookies from the oven, then transfer to a cooling rack and let cool. Meanwhile, heat the chocolate pieces in a heatproof bowl set over a pan of gently simmering water until melted. Stir the chocolate, then let cool slightly. Use a spoon to drizzle the chocolate in waves over the cookies, or spoon it into a pastry bag and pipe zigzag lines over the cookies. When the chocolate has set, store the cookies in an airtight container in the refrigerator until ready to serve.

hocolate dipped cookies

ingredients

MAKES 20

6 tbsp unsalted butter, plus
   extra for greasing
3 oz/85 g/$^1/_2$ cup raw brown
   sugar
1 egg
1 oz/25 g/scant $^1/_4$ cup
   wheatgerm
4 oz/115 g/generous $^3/_4$ cup
   whole-wheat
   self-rising flour
6 tbsp self-rising flour, sifted
4$^1/_2$ oz/130 g semisweet
   chocolate, broken into
   pieces

method

1 Beat the butter and sugar together in a bowl until fluffy. Add the egg and beat well. Stir in the wheatgerm and flours. Bring the mixture together with your hands.

2 Roll rounded teaspoons of the mixture into balls and place on 1–2 greased cookie sheets, spaced well apart to allow for spreading. Flatten the cookies slightly with a fork, then bake in a preheated oven, 350°F/180°C, for 15–20 minutes, or until golden.

3 Remove from the oven and let cool on the cookie sheets for a few minutes before transferring to a cooling rack to cool completely.

4 Melt the chocolate in a heatproof bowl set over a pan of gently simmering water, then dip each cookie in the chocolate to cover the base and a little way up the sides. Let the excess chocolate drip back into the bowl. Place the cookies on a sheet of parchment paper and let set in a cool place before serving.

white chocolate brownies

ingredients

MAKES 9

8 oz/225 g white chocolate

3 oz/85 g/³/₄ cup walnut
   pieces

4 oz/115 g unsalted butter,
   plus extra for greasing

2 eggs

4 oz/115 g/generous ¹/₂ cup
   soft brown sugar

3¹/₂ oz/100 g/generous
   ²/₃ cup self-rising flour

method

1 Coarsely chop 6 oz/175 g of white chocolate and all the walnuts. Put the remaining chocolate and the butter in a heatproof bowl set over a pan of gently simmering water. When melted, stir together, then set aside to cool slightly.

2 Whisk the eggs and sugar together, then beat in the cooled chocolate mixture until well mixed. Fold in the flour, chopped chocolate, and the walnuts. Turn the mixture into a lightly greased 7-inch/18-cm square cake pan and smooth the surface.

3 Transfer the pan to a preheated oven, 350°F/180°C, and bake for 30 minutes, or until just set. The mixture should still be a little soft in the center. Remove from the oven and let cool in the pan, then cut into 9 squares before serving.

pecan brownies

ingredients

MAKES 20

2^1/$_2$ oz/70 g bittersweet
   chocolate

^{1}/$_2$ oz/130 g/scant 1 cup
   all-purpose flour

^{3}/$_4$ tsp baking soda

^{1}/$_4$ tsp baking powder

1^1/$_2$ oz/40 g/^{1}/$_3$ cup pecans

8 oz/225 g unsalted butter,
   plus extra for greasing

2 oz/55 g/^{1}/$_2$ cup raw brown
   sugar

^{1}/$_2$ tsp almond extract

1 egg

1 tsp milk

method

1 Put the chocolate in a heatproof bowl set over a pan of gently simmering water and heat until it is melted. Meanwhile, sift together the flour, baking soda, and baking powder into a large bowl.

2 Finely chop the pecans and set aside. In a separate bowl, beat together the butter and sugar, then mix in the almond extract and the egg. Remove the chocolate from the heat and stir into the butter mixture. Add the flour mixture, milk, and chopped nuts to the bowl and stir until well combined.

3 Spoon the mixture into a large, greased baking dish lined with parchment paper and smooth it. Transfer to a preheated oven, 350°F/180°C, and cook for 30 minutes, or until firm to the touch (it should still be a little soft in the center). Remove from the oven and let cool completely. Cut into 20 squares and serve.

walnut & cinnamon blondies

ingredients

MAKES 9

4 oz/115 g unsalted butter,
 plus extra for greasing
8 oz/225 g/scant 1¹/₄ cups
 soft brown sugar
1 egg
1 egg yolk
5 oz/150 g/1 cup self-rising
 flour
1 tsp ground cinnamon
3 oz/85 g/³/₄ cup walnuts,
 coarsely chopped

method

1 Place the butter and sugar in a pan over low heat and stir until the sugar has dissolved. Cook, stirring, for 1 minute more. The mixture will bubble slightly, but do not let it boil. Let cool for 10 minutes.

2 Stir the egg and egg yolk into the mixture. Sift in the flour and cinnamon, then add the nuts and stir until just blended. Pour the cake mixture into a greased 7-inch/18-cm square cake pan lined with parchment paper and bake in a preheated oven, 350°F/180°C, for 20–25 minutes, or until springy in the middle and a toothpick inserted into the center comes out clean.

3 Let cool in the pan for a few minutes, then run a knife around the edge of the pan to loosen. Turn out onto a cooling rack and peel off the paper. Let cool completely. When cold, cut into squares.

walnut & chocolate chip slices

ingredients

MAKES 18

2 oz/55 g/1 cup walnut pieces

8 oz/225 g unsalted butter,
   plus extra for greasing

$3^1/2$ oz/100 g/scant 1 cup
   superfine sugar

few drops vanilla extract

8 oz/225 g/$1^1/2$ cups
   all-purpose flour

7 oz/200 g/scant $1^1/4$ cups
   bittersweet chocolate
   chips

method

1 Coarsely chop the walnut pieces to about the same size as the chocolate chips.

2 Beat the butter and sugar together until pale and fluffy. Add the vanilla extract, then stir in the flour. Stir in the walnuts and chocolate chips. Press the mixture into a greased 8 x 12-inch/20 x 30-cm jelly roll pan. Bake in a preheated oven, 350°F/180°C, for 20–25 minutes, or until golden brown. Remove from the oven. Cool in the pan and cut into slices.

strawberry & chocolate slices

ingredients

MAKES 16

8 oz/225 g/1¹/₂ cups all-
    purpose flour
1 tsp baking powder
3¹/₂ oz/100 g/¹/₂ cup
    superfine sugar
3 oz/85 g/scant ¹/₂ cup soft
    brown sugar
8 oz/225 g unsalted butter
6 oz/175 g/1 cup oatmeal
6 oz/175 g/²/₃ cup strawberry
    jelly
3¹/₂ oz/100 g/scant ²/₃ cup
    semisweet chocolate chips
1 oz/25 g/scant ¹/₄ cup
    almonds, chopped

method

1 Sift the flour and baking powder into a large mixing bowl.

2 Add the superfine sugar and brown sugar to the flour and mix well. Add the butter and rub in until the mixture resembles bread crumbs. Stir in the oatmeal.

3 Press three-quarters of the mixture into the bottom of a greased 12 x 8-inch/30 x 20-cm deep-sided jelly roll pan lined with parchment paper. Bake in a preheated oven, 375°F/190°C, for 10 minutes.

4 Spread the jelly over the cooked base, then sprinkle over the chocolate chips. Mix the remaining flour mixture with the almonds. Sprinkle evenly over the chocolate chips and press down gently.

5 Return to the oven and bake for an additional 20–25 minutes, or until golden brown. Remove from the oven and let cool in the pan, then cut into slices.

caramel chocolate shortbread

ingredients

MAKES 12

4 oz/115 g unsalted butter,
plus extra for greasing

6 oz/175 g/scant $1^1/4$ cups
all-purpose flour

$1^3/4$ oz/50 g/$^1/4$ cup golden
superfine sugar

filling and topping

7 oz/200 g butter

4 oz/115 g/generous $^1/2$ cup
golden superfine sugar

3 tbsp corn syrup

14 fl oz/400 ml canned
condensed milk

7 oz/200 g bittersweet
chocolate, broken into
pieces

method

1 Place the butter, flour, and sugar in a food processor and process until they begin to bind together. Press the mixture into a greased 9-inch/23-cm shallow square cake pan lined with parchment paper and smooth the top. Bake in a preheated oven, 350°F/180°C, for 20–25 minutes, or until golden.

2 Meanwhile, make the filling. Place the butter, sugar, syrup, and condensed milk in a pan and heat gently until the sugar has dissolved. Bring to a boil and simmer for 6–8 minutes, stirring constantly, until the mixture becomes very thick. Remove the shortbread from the oven, then pour over the filling and chill in the refrigerator until firm.

3 To make the topping, melt the chocolate in a heatproof bowl set over a pan of gently simmering water. Remove from the heat and let cool slightly, then spread over the caramel. Chill in the refrigerator until set. Cut into 12 pieces with a sharp knife and serve.

chocolate coconut layers

ingredients

MAKES 9

8 oz/225 g chocolate graham
   crackers

6 tbsp unsalted butter or
   margarine, plus extra for
   greasing

7 fl oz/200 ml/$^7/_8$ cup canned
   evaporated milk

1 egg, beaten

1 tsp vanilla extract

2 tbsp superfine sugar

1$^1/_2$ oz/40 g/scant $^1/_3$ cup
   self-rising flour, sifted

4 oz/115 g/scant 1$^1/_3$ cups
   dry unsweetened coconut

1$^3/_4$ oz/50 g semisweet
   chocolate (optional)

method

1 Crush the crackers in a plastic bag with a rolling pin or process them in a food processor. Melt the butter in a pan and stir in the crushed crackers thoroughly. Remove from the heat and press the mixture into the bottom of a shallow 8-inch/20-cm square cake pan lined with parchment paper.

2 In a separate bowl, beat together the evaporated milk, egg, vanilla, and sugar until smooth. Stir in the flour and coconut. Pour over the cracker layer and use a spatula to smooth the top.

3 Bake in a preheated oven, 375°F/190°C, for 30 minutes, or until the coconut topping has become firm and just golden. Remove from the oven and let cool in the cake pan for about 5 minutes, then cut into squares. Let cool completely in the pan.

4 Carefully remove the squares from the pan and place them on a cutting board. Melt the semisweet chocolate (if using) and drizzle it over the squares to decorate them. Let the chocolate set before serving.

chocolate peppermint slices

ingredients

SERVES 16

4 tbsp unsalted butter, plus extra for greasing

2 oz/55 g/$\frac{1}{4}$ cup superfine sugar

3$\frac{1}{2}$ oz/100 g/generous $\frac{2}{3}$ cup all-purpose flour

8 oz/225 g/1$\frac{1}{4}$ cups confectioners' sugar

1–2 tbsp warm water

$\frac{1}{2}$ tsp peppermint extract

6 oz/175 g bittersweet chocolate, broken into pieces

method

1 Beat the butter and sugar together until pale and fluffy. Stir in the flour until the mixture binds together.

2 Knead the mixture to form a smooth dough, then press into a greased 8 x 12-inch/20 x 30-cm jelly roll pan lined with parchment paper. Prick the surface all over with a fork. Bake in a preheated oven, 350°F/180°C, for 10–15 minutes, or until lightly browned and just firm to the touch. Remove from the oven and let cool in the pan.

3 Sift the confectioners' sugar into a bowl. Gradually add the water, then add the peppermint extract. Spread the frosting over the base, then let set.

4 Melt the chocolate in a heatproof bowl set over a pan of gently simmering water, then remove from the heat and spread over the frosting. Let set, then cut into slices.

pies & tarts

The person who invented pie dough deserves a word of thanks from us all, because without it we would never experience the pleasure of an incredible range of mouthwatering fillings encased in a crisp, delicous shell.

One of the tastiest ways to use pie dough is in a fruit pie. There are lots of ideas to choose from here, from the wonderful Traditional Apple Pie— be generous with the spices, both for aroma and taste—to the glorious Fig, Ricotta, and Honey Tart with its sunshine flavor of the Mediterranean. To ring the changes, try the Paper-thin Fruit Pies—the fruit nestles in a crisp "nest" of filo pastry—or the "upside-down" Peach and Preserved Ginger Tarte Tatin.

If you want something completely and utterly indulgent, try Chocolate Fudge Tart, served with a glass of your favorite dessert wine. This fabulous creation looks so elegant, yet is remarkably quick and easy to make. Crème Brûlée Tarts are double heaven—a really special dessert in its own right, the custard is even better served in a shell.

If you are in a hurry but still want to bake a pie, choose a recipe where you can use ready-made pie dough—you'll still have all the pleasure of rolling it out!

chocolate orange pie

ingredients

SERVES 4

pie dough

7 oz/200 g/scant 1^1/2 cups
   all-purpose flour, plus
   extra for dusting
3^1/2 oz/100 g butter, cut into
   small pieces, plus extra for
   greasing
2 oz/55 g/scant ^{1}/2 cup
   confectioners' sugar, sifted
finely grated rind of 1 orange
1 egg yolk, beaten
3 tbsp milk

filling

7 oz/200 g semisweet
   chocolate, broken into
   small pieces
2 eggs, separated
4 fl oz/125 ml/^{1}/2 cup milk
3^1/2 oz/100 g/^{1}/2 cup
   superfine sugar
8 amaretti cookies, crushed

orange cream

1 tbsp orange-flavored
   liqueur, such as Cointreau
1 tbsp finely grated orange
   rind, plus extra to decorate
4 fl oz/125 ml/^{1}/2 cup heavy
   cream

method

1 To make the pie dough, sift the flour into a bowl. Rub in the butter with the fingertips until the mixture resembles bread crumbs. Mix in the confectioners' sugar, orange rind, egg yolk, and milk. Turn out onto a lightly floured counter and knead briefly. Wrap the dough and let chill in the refrigerator for 30 minutes.

2 Roll out two-thirds of the pie dough to a thickness of ^{1}/4 inch/5 mm and use it to line a greased 9-inch/23-cm tart pan.

3 To make the filling, melt the chocolate in a heatproof bowl set over a pan of barely simmering water. Beat in the egg yolks, then the milk. Remove from the heat. In a separate, greasefree bowl, whisk the egg whites until stiff, then stir in the superfine sugar. Fold the egg whites into the chocolate mixture, then stir in the cookies. Spoon into the pastry shell.

4 Roll out the remaining pie dough, cut into strips, and use to form a lattice over the pie. Bake in a preheated oven, 350°F/180°C, for 1 hour.

5 To make the orange cream, beat the liqueur, orange rind, and cream together. Remove the pie from the oven, decorate with orange rind, and serve with the orange cream.

pecan pie

ingredients

SERVES 8

pie dough

9 oz/250 g/scant 1^5/$_8$ cups
    all-purpose flour
pinch of salt
4 oz/115 g butter, cut into
    small pieces
1 tbsp lard or vegetable
    shortening, cut into
    small pieces
2 oz/55 g/generous ^{1}/$_4$ cup
    golden superfine sugar
6 tbsp cold milk

filling

3 eggs
8 oz/250 g/generous 1 cup
    dark brown sugar
1 tsp vanilla extract
pinch of salt
3 oz/85 g butter, melted
3 tbsp corn syrup
3 tbsp molasses
12 oz/350 g/2 cups shelled
    pecans, roughly chopped

pecan halves, to decorate
whipped cream or vanilla ice
    cream, to serve

method

1 To make the pie dough, sift the flour and salt into a mixing bowl and rub in the butter and lard with the fingertips until the mixture resembles fine bread crumbs. Work in the superfine sugar and add the milk. Work the mixture into a soft dough. Wrap the dough and let chill in the refrigerator for 30 minutes.

2 Roll out the pie dough and use it to line a 9–10-inch/23–25-cm tart pan. Trim off the excess by running the rolling pin over the top of the tart pan. Line with parchment paper, and fill with dried beans. Bake in a preheated oven, 400°F/200°C, for 20 minutes. Take out of the oven and remove the paper and dried beans. Reduce the oven temperature to 350°F/180°C. Place a baking sheet in the oven.

3 To make the filling, place the eggs in a bowl and beat lightly. Beat in the dark brown sugar, vanilla extract, and salt. Stir in the butter, syrup, molasses, and chopped nuts. Pour into the pastry shell and decorate with the pecan halves.

4 Place on the heated baking sheet and bake in the oven for 35–40 minutes until the filling is set. Serve warm or at room temperature with whipped cream or vanilla ice cream.

mississippi mud pie

ingredients

SERVES 8

pie dough

9 oz/250 g/scant 1⅝ cups
all-purpose flour, plus
extra for dusting

2 tbsp unsweetened cocoa

5 oz/140 g butter

2 tbsp superfine sugar

1–2 tbsp cold water

filling

6 oz/175 g butter

9 oz/250 g/scant 1¾ cups
packed brown sugar

4 eggs, lightly beaten

4 tbsp unsweetened cocoa,
sifted

5½ oz/150 g semisweet
chocolate

10 fl oz/300 ml/1¼ cups
light cream

1 tsp chocolate extract

to decorate

15 fl oz/475 ml/scant 2 cups
heavy cream, whipped

chocolate flakes and curls

method

1 To make the pie dough, sift the flour and cocoa into a mixing bowl. Rub in the butter with the fingertips until the mixture resembles fine bread crumbs. Stir in the sugar and enough cold water to mix to a soft dough. Wrap the dough and let chill in the refrigerator for 15 minutes.

2 Roll out the dough on a lightly floured counter and use to line a 9-inch/23-cm loose-bottom tart pan or ceramic pie dish. Line with parchment paper and fill with dried beans. Bake in a preheated oven, 375°F/190°C, for 15 minutes. Remove from the oven and take out the paper and beans. Bake the pastry shell for an additional 10 minutes.

3 To make the filling, beat the butter and sugar together in a bowl and gradually beat in the eggs with the cocoa. Melt the chocolate and beat it into the mixture with the light cream and the chocolate extract.

4 Reduce the oven temperature to 325°F/160°C. Pour the mixture into the pastry shell and bake for 45 minutes, or until the filling has set gently. Let cool completely, then transfer to a serving plate.

5 Cover the mud pie with the whipped cream, decorate with chocolate flakes and curls, and let chill until ready to serve.

chocolate chiffon pie

ingredients

SERVES 8

nut base

8 oz/225 g/scant 2 cups
  shelled Brazil nuts
4 tbsp granulated sugar
4 tsp melted butter

filling

8 fl oz/225 ml/1 cup milk
2 tsp powdered gelatin
4 oz/115 g/generous $^1/_2$ cup
  superfine sugar
2 eggs, separated
8 oz/225 g semisweet
  chocolate, roughly chopped
1 tsp vanilla extract
5 fl oz/150 ml/$^2/_3$ cup
  heavy cream

2 tbsp chopped Brazil nuts,
  to decorate

method

1 To make the base, process the whole Brazil nuts in a food processor until finely ground. Add the sugar and melted butter and process briefly to combine. Tip the mixture into a 9-inch/23-cm round tart pan and press it onto the base and side with a spoon. Bake in a preheated oven, 400°F/200°C, for 8–10 minutes, or until light golden brown. Let cool.

2 Pour the milk into a bowl and sprinkle over the gelatin. Let it soften for 2 minutes, then set over a pan of gently simmering water. Stir in half of the superfine sugar, both the egg yolks, and all the chocolate. Stir constantly over low heat for 4–5 minutes until the gelatin has dissolved and the chocolate has melted. Remove from the heat and beat until the mixture is smooth. Stir in the vanilla extract, wrap, and let chill in the refrigerator for 45–60 minutes until starting to set.

3 Whip the cream until it is stiff, then fold all but 3 tablespoons into the chocolate mixture. Whisk the egg whites in a separate, clean, greasefree bowl until soft peaks form. Add 2 teaspoons of the remaining sugar and whisk until stiff peaks form. Fold in the remaining sugar, then fold the egg whites into the chocolate mixture. Pour the filling into the pastry shell and let chill in the refrigerator for 3 hours. Decorate with the remaining whipped cream and the chopped nuts before serving.

custard pie

ingredients

SERVES 8

pie dough

7 oz/200 g/scant $1^1/4$ cups
    all-purpose flour
2 tbsp superfine sugar
4 oz/115 g butter,
    cut into small pieces
1 tbsp water

filling

3 eggs
3 oz/85 g/$^1/_3$ cup
    superfine sugar
5 fl oz/150 ml/$^2/_3$ cup
    light cream
5 fl oz/150 ml/$^2/_3$ cup milk
freshly grated nutmeg

whipped cream (optional),
    to serve

method

1 To make the pie dough, place the flour and sugar in a mixing bowl. Rub in the butter with the fingertips until the mixture resembles fine bread crumbs. Add the water and mix together until a soft dough has formed. Wrap the dough and let chill in the refrigerator for 30 minutes, then roll out to a circle slightly larger than a $9^1/2$-inch/24-cm loose-bottom tart pan.

2 Line the pan with the dough, trimming off the edge. Prick all over the base with a fork and let chill in the refrigerator for about 30 minutes.

3 Line the pastry shell with parchment paper and fill with dried beans. Bake in a preheated oven, 375°F/190°C, for 15 minutes. Remove the paper and beans and bake the pastry shell for an additional 15 minutes.

4 To make the filling, whisk the eggs, sugar, cream, milk, and nutmeg together. Pour the filling into the prepared pastry shell.

5 Return the pie to the oven and cook for an additional 25–30 minutes, or until the filling is just set. Serve with whipped cream, if you like.

pumpkin pie

ingredients

SERVES 6

4 lb/1.8 kg sweet pumpkin, halved and the stem, seeds, and stringy insides removed and discarded

5 oz/150 g/1 cup all-purpose flour, plus extra for dusting

$1/4$ tsp baking powder

1 tsp salt

$1^1/2$ tsp ground cinnamon

$3/4$ tsp ground nutmeg

$3/4$ tsp ground cloves

$1^3/4$ oz/50 g/$1/4$ cup superfine sugar

4 tbsp unsalted butter, diced, plus extra for greasing

3 eggs

14 fl oz/425 ml/$1^3/4$ cups sweetened condensed milk

$1/2$ tsp vanilla extract

1 tbsp raw sugar

streusel topping

2 tbsp all-purpose flour

4 tbsp raw sugar

1 tsp ground cinnamon

2 tbsp cold unsalted butter, in small pieces

3 oz/55 g/generous $2/3$ cup shelled pecans, chopped

3 oz/55 g/generous $2/3$ cup shelled walnuts, chopped

method

1 Place the pumpkin halves, face down, in a baking pan and cover with foil. Bake in a preheated oven, 375°F/190°C, for $1^1/2$ hours, then remove and let cool. Purée the flesh in a food processor, drain away any excess liquid, then cover with plastic wrap and let chill.

2 To make the pie dough, sift the flour and baking powder into a bowl with $1/2$ teaspoon each of salt and cinnamon and $1/4$ teaspoon each of nutmeg and cloves. Add the superfine sugar and rub in the butter until the mixture resembles fine bread crumbs. Add 1 egg, lightly beaten, and mix to a soft dough. Roll out the dough on a lightly floured counter, use to line a greased 9-inch/23-cm round pie dish, then trim the edge. Cover with plastic wrap and let chill for 30 minutes.

3 To make the filling, place the pumpkin purée in a bowl, then stir in the condensed milk and remaining eggs. Add the remaining spices and salt, then stir in the vanilla extract and raw sugar. Pour into the pastry shell and bake in a preheated oven, 425°F/220°C, for 15 minutes.

4 Meanwhile, make the topping. Combine the flour, sugar, and cinnamon in a bowl, rub in the butter until crumbly, then stir in the nuts. Remove the pie from the oven and reduce the heat to 350°F/180°C. Sprinkle over the topping, bake for 35 minutes, and serve hot or cold.

forest fruit pie

ingredients

SERVES 4

filling

8 oz/225 g/1⅝ cups
   blueberries
8 oz/225 g/1⅝ cups
   raspberries
8 oz/225 g/1⅝ cups
   blackberries
1½ oz/45 g/⅓ cup superfine
   sugar
2 tbsp confectioners' sugar,
   to decorate

pie dough

8 oz/225 g/scant 1⅜ cups
   all-purpose flour, plus
   extra for dusting
1 oz/25 g/generous ¼ cup
   ground hazelnuts
3½ oz/100 g butter, cut into
   small pieces, plus extra
   for greasing
2 oz/55 g/⅔ cup superfine
   sugar
finely grated rind of 1 lemon
1 egg yolk, beaten
4 tbsp milk

whipped cream, to serve

method

1 Place the fruit in a pan with 3 tablespoons of the superfine sugar and let simmer gently, stirring frequently, for 5 minutes. Remove the pan from the heat.

2 Sift the flour into a bowl, then add the hazelnuts. Rub in the butter with the fingertips until the mixture resembles bread crumbs, then sift in the remaining sugar. Add the lemon rind, egg yolk, and 3 tablespoons of the milk and mix. Turn out onto a lightly floured counter and knead briefly. Wrap and let chill in the refrigerator for 30 minutes.

3 Grease an 8-inch/20-cm pie dish with butter. Roll out two-thirds of the pie dough to a thickness of ¼ inch/5 mm and use it to line the base and side of the dish. Spoon the fruit into the pastry shell. Brush the rim with water, then roll out the remaining pie dough to cover the pie. Trim and crimp round the edge, then make 2 small slits in the top and decorate with 2 leaf shapes cut out from the dough trimmings. Brush all over with the remaining milk. Bake in a preheated oven, 375°F/190°C, for 40 minutes.

4 Remove from the oven, sprinkle with the confectioners' sugar, and serve with whipped cream.

traditional apple pie

ingredients

SERVES 6

pie dough

12 oz/350 g/generous
  2³/₈ cups all-purpose flour
pinch of salt
3 oz/85 g butter or margarine,
  cut into small pieces
3 oz/85 g lard or vegetable
  shortening, cut into
  small pieces
about 6 tbsp cold water
beaten egg or milk, for glazing

filling

1 lb 10 oz–2 lb 4 oz/750 g–1 kg
  cooking apples, peeled,
  cored, and sliced
4 oz/115 g/scant ²/₃ cup
  packed brown or superfine
  sugar, plus extra
  for sprinkling
¹/₂–1 tsp ground cinnamon,
  allspice, or ground ginger
1–2 tbsp water (optional)

whipped heavy cream,
  to serve

method

1 To make the pie dough, sift the flour and salt into a large bowl. Add the butter and fat and rub in with the fingertips until the mixture resembles fine bread crumbs. Add the water and gather the mixture together into a dough. Wrap the dough and let chill in the refrigerator for 30 minutes.

2 Roll out almost two-thirds of the pie dough thinly and use to line a deep 9-inch/23-cm pie plate or pie pan.

3 Mix the apples with the sugar and spice and pack into the pastry shell; the filling can come up above the rim. Add the water if needed, particularly if the apples are a dry variety.

4 Roll out the remaining pie dough to form a lid. Dampen the edges of the pie rim with water and position the lid, pressing the edges firmly together. Trim and crimp the edges.

5 Use the trimmings to cut out leaves or other shapes to decorate the top of the pie, dampen and attach. Glaze the top of the pie with beaten egg or milk, make 1–2 slits in the top, and place the pie on a baking sheet.

6 Bake in a preheated oven, 425°F/220°C, for 20 minutes, then reduce the temperature to 350°F/180°C and bake for an additional 30 minutes, or until the pastry is a light golden brown. Serve hot or cold, sprinkled with sugar, with whipped cream.

apple lattice pie

ingredients

SERVES 4

pie dough

10 oz/280 g/2 cups
   all-purpose flour,
   plus extra for dusting
pinch of salt
2 oz/50 g/$\frac{1}{4}$ cup
   superfine sugar
9 oz/250 g butter,
   cut into small pieces
1 egg
1 egg yolk
1 tbsp water

filling

3 tbsp black currant or
   plum jelly
2 oz/55 g/generous $\frac{3}{8}$ cup
   chopped toasted
   mixed nuts
2 lb 2 oz/950 g cooking apples
1 tbsp lemon juice
1 tsp apple pie spice
2 oz/55 g/$\frac{3}{8}$ cup
   golden raisins
1$\frac{3}{4}$ oz/50 g grapes,
   halved and seeded
2$\frac{3}{4}$ oz/75 g/generous $\frac{1}{3}$ cup
   packed brown sugar

confectioners' sugar,
   for dusting
custard, to serve

method

1 To make the pie dough, sift the flour and salt into a bowl. Make a well in the center and add the sugar, butter, egg, egg yolk, and water. Mix together to form a smooth dough, adding more water if necessary. Wrap the dough and let chill in the refrigerator for 1 hour.

2 Shape about three-quarters of the dough into a ball and roll out on a lightly floured counter into a circle large enough to line a shallow 10-inch/25-cm tart pan. Fit it into the pan and trim the edge. Roll out the remaining pie dough and cut into long strips about $\frac{1}{2}$ inch/1 cm wide.

3 To make the filling, spread the jelly evenly over the base of the pastry shell, then sprinkle over the toasted nuts. Peel and core the apples, then cut them into thin slices. Place them in a bowl with the lemon juice, apple pie spice, golden raisins, grapes, and brown sugar. Mix together gently. Spoon the mixture into the pastry shell, spreading it out evenly.

4 Arrange the pie dough strips in a lattice over the top of the pie. Moisten with a little water, seal, and trim the edges. Bake in a preheated oven, 400°F/200°C, for 50 minutes until golden. Dust with confectioners' sugar. Serve at once with custard.

pear pie

ingredients

SERVES 6

pie dough

10 oz/280 g/scant 2 cups
      all-purpose flour
pinch of salt
4 oz/115 g/scant $^2/_3$ cup
      superfine sugar
4 oz/115 g butter,
      cut into small pieces
1 egg
1 egg yolk
few drops vanilla extract
2–3 tsp water

filling

4 tbsp apricot jelly
2 oz/55 g Amaretti or Ratafia
      cookies, crumbled
1 lb 14 oz–2 lb 4 oz/850 g–1 kg
      pears, peeled and cored
1 tsp ground cinnamon
3 oz/85 g/$^1/_2$ cup raisins
3 oz/85 g/$^1/_3$ cup packed
      brown or raw sugar

sifted confectioners' sugar,
      for sprinkling

method

1 To make the dough, sift the flour and salt onto a counter, make a well in the center, and add the sugar, butter, egg, egg yolk, vanilla extract, and most of the water. Using your fingers, gradually work the flour into the other ingredients to form a smooth dough, adding more water if necessary. Wrap the dough and let chill in the refrigerator for at least 1 hour.

2 Roll out three-quarters of the dough and use to line a shallow 10-inch/25-cm cake pan or deep tart pan.

3 To make the filling, spread the jelly over the base and sprinkle with the crushed cookies. Slice the pears very thinly. Arrange over the cookies in the pastry shell. Sprinkle with cinnamon, then with raisins, and finally with brown sugar.

4 Roll out a thin sausage shape using one-third of the remaining pie dough, and place around the edge of the pie. Roll the remainder into thin sausages and arrange in a lattice over the pie, 4 or 5 strips in each direction, attaching them to the strip around the edge.

5 Cook in a preheated oven, 400°F/200°C, for 50 minutes until golden brown and cooked through. Let cool, then serve warm or chilled, sprinkled with sifted confectioners' sugar.

lemon meringue pie

ingredients

SERVES 4

pie dough

6 oz/185 g/generous 1 cup
    all-purpose flour, plus
    extra for dusting
3 oz/85 g butter, cut into
    small pieces, plus extra
    for greasing
2 oz/55 g/$1/4$ cup
    confectioners' sugar, sifted
finely grated rind of $1/2$ lemon
$1/2$ egg yolk, beaten
$1^1/2$ tbsp milk

filling

3 tbsp cornstarch
10 fl oz/300 ml/$1^1/4$ cups
    water
juice and grated
    rind of 2 lemons
6 oz/185 g/generous $3/4$ cup
    superfine sugar
2 eggs, separated

method

1 To make the pie dough, sift the flour into a bowl. Rub in the butter with the fingertips until the mixture resembles fine bread crumbs. Mix in the remaining ingredients. Knead briefly on a lightly floured counter. Let rest for 30 minutes.

2 Grease an 8-inch/20-cm pie dish with butter. Roll out the pie dough to a thickness of $1/4$ inch/ 5 mm; use it to line the base and sides of the dish. Prick all over with a fork, line with parchment paper, and fill with dried beans. Preheat the oven to 350°F/180°C and bake for 15 minutes. Remove from the oven and take out the paper and beans. Reduce the temperature to 300°F/150°C.

3 To make the filling, mix the cornstarch with a little of the water. Place the remaining water in a pan. Stir in the lemon juice and rind and cornstarch paste. Bring to a boil, stirring. Cook for 2 minutes. Let cool a little. Stir in 5 tablespoons of the sugar and the egg yolks and pour into the pastry shell.

4 Whisk the egg whites in a clean, greasefree bowl until stiff. Whisk in the remaining sugar and spread over the pie. Bake for another 40 minutes. Remove from the oven, let cool, and serve.

paper-thin fruit pies

ingredients

MAKES 4

1 eating apple

1 ripe pear

2 tbsp lemon juice

4 tbsp melted butter

4 sheets filo pastry,
    thawed if frozen

2 tbsp apricot jelly

1 tbsp unsweetened
    orange juice

1 tbsp finely chopped
    pistachios

2 tsp confectioners' sugar,
    for dusting

method

1 Core and thinly slice the apple and pear and immediately toss them in the lemon juice to prevent them from turning brown. Melt the butter in a pan over low heat.

2 Cut each sheet of pastry into 4 and cover with a clean, damp dish towel. Brush a 4-cup nonstick muffin pan (cup size 4 inches/ 10 cm in diameter) with a little of the butter.

3 Brush 4 small sheets of pastry with melted butter. Press a sheet of pastry into the base of 1 cup. Arrange the other sheets of pastry on top at slightly different angles. Repeat with the other sheets of pastry to make another 3 pies.

4 Arrange alternate slices of apple and pear in the center of each pie shell and lightly crimp the edges of the pastry.

5 Stir the jelly and orange juice together until smooth and brush over the fruit. Bake in a preheated oven, 400°F/200°C, for 12–15 minutes. Sprinkle with the pistachios, dust lightly with confectioners' sugar, and serve hot straight from the oven.

maple pecan pies

ingredients

MAKES 12

pie dough

5 oz/150 g/1 cup all-purpose
  flour, plus extra for dusting
3 oz/85 g butter, cut into
  small pieces
2 oz/55 g/generous $^1/_4$ cup
  golden superfine sugar
2 egg yolks

filling

2 tbsp maple syrup
5 fl oz/150 ml/$^2/_3$ cup
  heavy cream
4 oz/115 g/$^2/_3$ cup golden
  superfine sugar
pinch of cream of tartar
6 tbsp water
6 oz/185 g/1 cup shelled
  pecans, chopped
12 pecan halves

method

1 To make the pie dough, sift the flour into a mixing bowl and rub in the butter with the fingertips until the mixture resembles bread crumbs. Add the sugar and egg yolks and mix to form a soft dough. Wrap the dough and let chill in the refrigerator for 30 minutes.

2 On a lightly floured counter, roll out the pie dough thinly, cut out 12 circles, and use to line 12 tartlet pans. Prick the bases with a fork. Line with parchment paper and fill with dried beans. Bake in a preheated oven, 400°F/200°C, for 10–15 minutes, until light golden. Remove from the oven and take out the paper and beans. Bake the pastry shells for 2–3 minutes more. Let cool on a wire rack.

3 Mix half the maple syrup and half the cream in a bowl. Place the sugar, cream of tartar, and water in a pan and heat gently until the sugar dissolves. Bring to a boil and boil until light golden. Remove from the heat and stir in the maple syrup and cream mixture.

4 Return the pan to the heat and cook until a little of the mixture dropped into a bowl of cold water forms a soft ball. Stir in the remaining cream and leave until cool. Brush the remaining maple syrup over the edges of the pies. Place the chopped pecans in the pastry shells and spoon in the toffee. Top each pie with a pecan half. Let cool completely before serving.

fig, ricotta & honey tart

ingredients

SERVES 6

pie dough

$2^1/_2$ oz/75 g cold butter,
    cut into pieces, plus extra
    for greasing
5 oz/150 g/generous $^3/_4$ cup
    all-purpose flour
pinch of salt
1 oz/25 g/scant $^1/_3$ cup
    ground almonds
cold water

filling

6 figs
20 fl oz/600 ml/$2^1/_2$ cups
    water
$3^1/_2$ oz/100 g/$^1/_2$ cup
    superfine sugar
4 egg yolks
$^1/_2$ tsp vanilla extract
1 lb 2 oz/500 g ricotta
    cheese, drained of
    any liquid
2 tbsp flower honey, plus
    1 tsp for drizzling

method

1 Lightly grease a 9-inch/23-cm loose-bottom fluted tart pan. Sift the flour and salt into a food processor, add the butter, and process until the mixture resembles fine bread crumbs. Tip the mixture into a bowl, stir in the almonds, and add just enough cold water to bring the dough together. Turn out onto a floured counter and roll out the dough $3^1/4$ inches/ 8 cm larger than the pan. Carefully lift the dough into the pan and press to fit. Roll the rolling pin over the pan to neaten the edges and trim the excess dough. Fit a piece of parchment paper into the tart shell, fill with dried beans, and let chill for 30 minutes.

2 Remove the pastry shell from the refrigerator and bake the tart shell blind for 15 minutes in a preheated oven, 375°F/190°C, then remove the beans and paper. Return to the oven for an additional 5 minutes.

3 Put the figs, half the superfine sugar, and the water in a pan and bring to a boil. Poach gently for 10 minutes, drain, and let cool. Stir the egg yolks and vanilla extract into the ricotta, add the remaining sugar and the honey, and mix well. Spoon into the tart shell and bake for 30 minutes. Remove from the oven and, when you are ready to serve, cut the figs in half lengthwise and arrange on the tart, cut-side up. Drizzle with the extra honey and serve at once.

honey & lemon tart

ingredients

SERVES 8–12

pastry shell

8 oz/225 g/1½ cups plus
   3 tbsp all-purpose flour
pinch of salt
1½ tsp superfine sugar
5½ oz/150 g butter
3-4 tbsp cold water

filling

13 oz/375 g/1⅓ cups cottage
   cheese, cream cheese,
   or ricotta
6 tbsp Greek honey
3 eggs, beaten
½ tsp cinnamon
grated rind and
   juice of 1 lemon

method

1 To make the pastry, put the flour, salt, sugar, and butter, cut into cubes, in a food processor. Mix in short bursts, until the mixture resembles fine bread crumbs. Sprinkle over the water and mix until the mixture forms a smooth dough. Alternatively, make the pastry in a bowl and rub in with your hands. The pastry can be used right away, but is better if allowed to rest in the refrigerator, wrapped in waxed paper or foil, for about 30 minutes before use.

2 Meanwhile, make the filling. (If using cottage cheese, push the cheese through a strainer into a bowl.) Add the honey to the cheese and beat until smooth. Add the eggs, cinnamon, and the lemon rind and juice, and mix well.

3 On a lightly floured surface, roll out the pastry and use to line a 9-inch/23-cm tart pan. Line with parchment paper, fill with dried beans, place on a baking sheet and bake in a preheated oven, 400°F/200°C, for 15 minutes. Remove from the oven, take out the parchment paper and beans, return to the oven and bake for another 5 minutes, until the base is firm but not brown.

4 Reduce the oven temperature to 350°F/180°C. Pour the filling into the pastry shell and bake in the oven for about 30 minutes until set. Serve cold.

plum & almond tart

ingredients

SERVES 8

butter, for greasing
all-purpose flour, for dusting
14 oz/400 g ready-made
    sweet pie dough

filling

1 egg
1 egg yolk
5 oz/140 g/scant $^3/_4$ cup
    golden superfine sugar
2 oz/55 g butter, melted
$3^1/_2$ oz/100 g/generous 1 cup
    ground almonds
1 tbsp brandy
2 lb/900 g plums,
    halved and pitted

whipped cream, to serve
    (optional)

method

1 Grease a 9-inch/23-cm tart pan. On a lightly floured counter, roll out the pastry and use it to line the tart pan, then bake blind. Place a baking sheet in the oven.

2 To make the filling, place the egg, egg yolk, $3^1/_2$ oz/100g/$^1/_2$ cup of the superfine sugar, melted butter, ground almonds, and brandy in a bowl and mix together to form a paste. Spread the paste in the tart shell.

3 Arrange the plum halves, cut-side up, on top of the almond paste, fitting them together tightly. Sprinkle with the remaining superfine sugar. Place the tart pan on the preheated cookie sheet and bake in a preheated oven, 400°F/200°C, for 35–40 minutes, or until the filling is set and the tart shell is brown. Serve warm with whipped cream, if you like.

bakewell tart

ingredients

SERVES 4

pie dough

5 oz/150 g/generous 1 cup
   all-purpose flour,
   plus extra for dusting
1³/4 oz/50 g butter, cut into
   small pieces, plus extra
   for greasing
1 oz/25 g/¹/4 cup
   confectioners' sugar, sifted
finely grated rind of ¹/2 lemon
¹/2 egg yolk, beaten
1¹/2 tbsp milk
4 tbsp strawberry jelly

filling

3¹/2 oz/100 g butter
3¹/2 oz/100 g/¹/2 cup
   packed brown sugar
2 eggs, beaten
1 tsp almond extract
4 oz/115 g/³/4 cup rice flour
3 tbsp ground almonds
3 tbsp slivered almonds,
   toasted

confectioners' sugar,
   to decorate

method

1 To make the pie dough, sift the flour into a bowl. Rub in the butter with the fingertips until the mixture resembles fine bread crumbs. Mix in the confectioners' sugar, lemon rind, egg yolk, and milk. Knead briefly on a lightly floured counter. Wrap the dough and let chill in the refrigerator for 30 minutes.

2 Grease an 8-inch/20-cm ovenproof tart pan. Roll out the pie dough to a thickness of ¹/4 inch/5 mm and use it to line the base and side of the pan. Prick all over the base with a fork, then spread with the jelly.

3 To make the filling, cream the butter and sugar together until fluffy. Gradually beat in the eggs, followed by the almond extract, rice flour, and ground almonds. Spread the mixture evenly over the jelly-covered pie dough, then sprinkle over the slivered almonds. Bake in a preheated oven, 375°F/ 190°C, for 40 minutes until golden. Remove from the oven, dust with confectioners' sugar, and serve warm.

almond tart

ingredients

SERVES 8–12

pie dough

10 oz/280 g/2 cups
    all-purpose flour
$5^1/_2$ oz/150 g generous
    $^3/_4$ cup superfine sugar
1 tsp finely grated lemon rind
pinch of salt
$5^1/_2$ oz/150 g unsalted butter,
    chilled and cut into
    small dice
1 medium egg, beaten lightly
1 tbsp chilled water

filling

6 oz/175 g unsalted butter,
    at room temperature
6 oz/175 g/scant $^7/_8$ cup
    superfine sugar
3 large eggs
6 oz/175 g/generous
    $1^1/_2$ cups finely
    ground almonds
2 tsp all-purpose flour
1 tbsp finely grated orange rind
$^1/_2$ tsp almond extract

confectioners' sugar,
    to decorate
sour cream (optional), to serve

method

1 First, make the pie dough. Put the flour, sugar, lemon rind, and salt in a bowl. Rub or cut in the butter until the mixture resembles fine bread crumbs. Combine the egg and water, then slowly pour into the flour, stirring with a fork until a coarse mass forms. Shape into a ball and let chill for at least 1 hour.

2 Roll out the pie dough on a lightly floured counter until $^1/_8$ inch/3 mm thick. Use to line a greased loose-bottom 10-inch/25-cm tart pan. Return the tart pan to the fridge for at least 15 minutes.

3 Cover the pastry shell with parchment paper and fill with dried beans. Bake in a preheated oven, 425°F/220°C, for 12 minutes. Remove the beans and parchment paper and return the pastry shell to the oven for 4 minutes to dry the base. Remove from the oven and reduce the oven temperature to 400°F/200°C.

4 To make the filling, beat the butter and sugar until creamy. Beat in the eggs, one at a time. Add the almonds, flour, orange rind, and almond extract, and beat until blended. Spoon into the pastry shell and smooth the surface. Bake for 30–35 minutes until the top is golden and the tip of a knife inserted in the center comes out clean. Let cool completely on a wire rack, then dust with confectioners' sugar. Serve with a spoonful of sour cream, if you like.

coconut tart

ingredients

SERVES 8

butter, for greasing

all-purpose flour, for dusting

14 oz/400 g ready-made
   sweet pie dough

filling

2 eggs

grated rind and
   juice of 2 lemons

7 oz/200 g/1 cup golden
   superfine sugar

13 fl oz/400 ml/1$\frac{2}{3}$ cups
   heavy cream

9 oz/250 g/2$\frac{3}{4}$ cups dry
   unsweetened coconut

method

1 Preheat the oven to 400°F/200°C, then grease a 9-inch/23-cm tart pan. On a lightly floured counter, roll out the pastry and use it to line the prepared pan, then bake blind. Reduce the oven temperature to 325°F/160°C and place a baking sheet in the oven.

2 To make the filling, place the eggs, lemon rind, and sugar in a bowl and beat together for 1 minute. Gently stir in the cream, then the lemon juice, and finally the coconut.

3 Spoon the filling into the tart shell and place the tart pan on the preheated baking sheet. Bake in the oven for 40 minutes, or until set and golden. Let cool for 1 hour to firm up. Serve at room temperature.

caramelized lemon tart

ingredients

SERVES 6

pie dough

3¹/2 oz/100 g cold butter,
    cut into pieces, plus extra
    for greasing
7 oz/200 g/1¹/8 cups
    all-purpose flour
pinch of salt
2 tbsp superfine sugar
1 egg yolk
cold water

filling

5 lemons
2 eggs
10 oz/275 g/1¹/2 cups
    superfine sugar
6 oz/175 g/generous
    1¹/2 cups ground almonds
4 fl oz/125 ml/¹/2 cup heavy
    whipping cream, whipped
3¹/2 fl oz/100 ml/generous
    ¹/3 cup water

heavy whipping cream,
    whipped, to serve

method

1 Lightly grease a 9-inch/23-cm loose-bottom fluted tart pan. Sift the flour and salt into a food processor, add the butter, and process until the mixture resembles fine bread crumbs. Tip the mixture into a large bowl, then add the sugar and egg yolk, and just enough cold water to bring the dough together. Roll out the dough on a lightly floured counter to a circle 3¹/4 inches/8 cm larger than the pan. Lift the dough carefully into the pan, press to fit, and trim the excess dough. Fit parchment paper into the tart shell and fill with dried beans. Let chill in the refrigerator for 30 minutes, then bake blind for 10 minutes in a preheated oven, 375°F/190°C. Remove the beans and paper and bake for 5 minutes more.

2 Put the juice and finely grated rind of 3 of the lemons in a bowl. Add the eggs, 3 oz/85 g/¹/2 cup of the sugar, the ground almonds, and the cream, whisking to combine. Pour into the pastry shell and bake for 25 minutes.

3 Thinly slice the remaining 2 lemons, discarding the seeds and ends. Heat the remaining sugar and the water in a pan until the sugar is dissolved. Let simmer for 5 minutes, then add the lemon slices and boil for 10 minutes. Arrange the lemon slices over the surface of the cooked tart. Drizzle over the remaining lemon syrup. Serve warm or cold, with whipped cream.

peach &
preserved ginger tarte tatin

ingredients

SERVES 6

9 oz/250 g ready-made
   puff pastry

filling

6–8 just ripe peaches

$3^{1}/_{2}$ oz/100 g/scant $^{1}/_{2}$ cup
   golden superfine sugar

3 heaping tbsp unsalted butter

3 pieces preserved ginger in
   syrup, chopped

1 tbsp ginger syrup from the
   preserved ginger jar

1 egg, beaten

method

1 Plunge the peaches into boiling water, then let drain and peel. Cut each in half. Put the sugar in a 10-inch/25-cm heavy, ovenproof skillet and heat it gently until it caramelizes. Don't stir, just shake the skillet if necessary. Once the sugar turns a dark caramel color, remove from the heat, and drop 2 tbsp of the butter into it.

2 Place the peaches cut-side up on top of the caramel, packing them as close together as possible, and tucking the preserved ginger pieces into any gaps. Dot with the remaining butter and drizzle with the ginger syrup.

3 Return to gentle heat while you roll out the dough in a circle larger than the skillet you are using. Drape the dough over the peaches and tuck it in well round the edges, brush with the beaten egg, and bake in a preheated oven, 375°F/190°C, for 20–25 minutes, until the pastry is browned and puffed up. Remove from the oven and let rest for 5 minutes, then invert onto a serving plate and serve.

walnut custard tarts

ingredients

SERVES 4

$1^{1}/_{2}$ oz/40 g/$^{1}/_{8}$ cup butter

8 sheets filo pastry (work with one sheet at a time and keep the remaining sheets covered with a damp dish towel)

$1^{1}/_{2}$ oz/40 g/$^{1}/_{4}$ cup walnut halves

5 oz/150 g/scant $^{2}/_{3}$ cup Greek yogurt

4 tbsp honey

5 fl oz/150 ml/$^{2}/_{3}$ cup heavy cream

2 tbsp superfine sugar

2 eggs

1 tsp vanilla extract

confectioners' sugar, for dusting

Greek yogurt, to serve (optional)

method

1 Melt the butter. Brush 4 deep 4-inch/ 10-cm tartlet pans with a little of the butter. Cut the sheets of filo pastry in half to make 16 rough squares.

2 Take 1 square of pastry, brush it with a little of the melted butter, and use it to line 1 of the pans. Repeat with 3 more pastry squares, placing each of them at a different angle. Line the remaining 3 pans and place the tins on a baking tray.

3 To make the filling, finely chop 2 tablespoons of the walnuts. Put the yogurt, honey, cream, sugar, eggs, and vanilla extract in a bowl and beat together. Stir in the chopped walnuts until well mixed.

4 Pour the yogurt filling into the pastry shells. Coarsely break the remaining walnuts and scatter over the top. Bake in a preheated oven, 350°F/180°C, for 25–30 minutes until the filling is firm to the touch.

5 Let the tartlets cool, then carefully remove from the pans and dust with confectioners' sugar. Serve with a bowl of yogurt, if desired.

chocolate fudge tart

ingredients

SERVES 6–8

flour, for sprinkling

12 oz/350 g ready-made
    unsweetened pie dough

confectioners' sugar, for dusting

filling

5 oz/140 g semisweet
    chocolate, finely chopped

6 oz/175 g butter, diced

12 oz/350 g/1¾ cups golden
    granulated sugar

3½ oz/100 g/¾ cup
    all-purpose flour

½ tsp vanilla extract

6 eggs, beaten

5 fl oz/150 ml/⅔ cup heavy
    whipping cream, whipped,
    and ground cinnamon,
    to decorate

method

1 Roll out the pie dough on a lightly floured counter and use to line an 8-inch/20-cm deep loose-bottom tart pan. Prick the dough base lightly with a fork, then line with parchment paper and fill with dried beans. Bake in a preheated oven, 400°F/200°C, for 12–15 minutes, or until the dough no longer looks raw. Remove from the oven, take out the beans and paper, return to the oven and bake for 10 minutes more, or until the dough is firm. Let cool. Reduce the oven temperature to 350°F/180°C.

2 To make the filling, place the chocolate and butter in a heatproof bowl and melt over a pan of gently simmering water. Stir until smooth, then remove from the heat and let cool. Place the sugar, flour, vanilla extract, and eggs in a separate bowl and whisk until well blended. Stir in the butter and chocolate mixture.

3 Pour the filling into the pastry shell and bake in the oven for 50 minutes, or until the filling is just set. Transfer to a wire rack to cool completely. Dust with confectioners' sugar before serving with whipped cream sprinkled lightly with cinnamon.

crème brûlée tarts

ingredients

SERVES 6

pie dough

5$\frac{1}{2}$ oz/150 g/1 cup
  all-purpose flour,
  plus extra for dusting
1–2 tbsp superfine sugar
4$\frac{1}{2}$ oz/125 g butter,
  cut into pieces
1 tbsp water

filling

4 egg yolks
1$\frac{1}{2}$ oz/50 g/$\frac{3}{4}$ cup
  superfine sugar
14 fl oz/425 ml/1$\frac{3}{4}$ cups
  heavy cream
1 tsp vanilla extract
raw brown sugar, for sprinkling

red currants and raspberries,
  to serve

method

1 To make the pie dough, place the flour and sugar in a large bowl. Rub in the butter with your fingertips until the mixture resembles bread crumbs. Add the water and mix to form a soft dough. Wrap and chill for 30 minutes.

2 Divide the dough into 6 pieces. Roll out each piece on a lightly floured counter to line 6 tart pans 4 inches/10 cm wide. Prick the bottom of the pastry with a fork and chill for 20 minutes.

3 Line the pastry shells with parchment paper and dried beans and bake in a preheated oven, 375°F/190°C, for 15 minutes. Remove the paper and beans and cook the pastry shells for an additional 10 minutes, or until crisp. Let cool.

4 To make the filling, beat the egg yolks and sugar together in a bowl until pale. Heat the cream and vanilla extract in a pan until just below boiling point, then pour it onto the egg mixture, whisking constantly. Return the mixture to a clean pan and bring to just below a boil, stirring, until thick. Do not allow the mixture to boil or it will curdle. Let cool slightly, then pour it into the tart pans. Let cool, then chill overnight.

5 Preheat the broiler. Sprinkle the tarts with the sugar. Cook under the hot broiler for a few minutes. Let cool, then let chill for 2 hours before serving with red currants and raspberries.

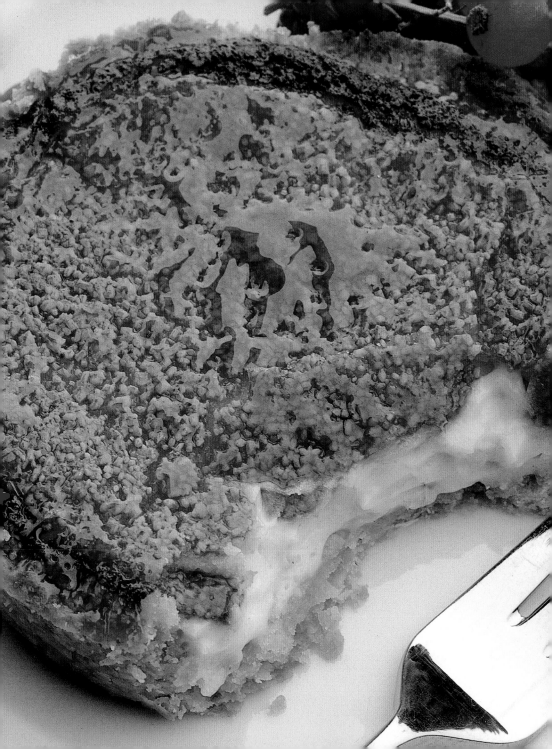

summer fruit tartlets

ingredients

MAKES 12

dough

7 oz/200 g/scant 1¹/₂ cups
    all-purpose flour, plus
    extra for dusting
3 oz/85 g/generous ³/₄ cup
    confectioners' sugar
2 oz/55 g/²/₃ cup
    ground almonds
4 oz/115 g butter
1 egg yolk
1 tbsp milk

filling

8 oz/225 g/1 cup
    cream cheese
confectioners' sugar, to taste,
    plus extra for dusting
12 oz/350 g fresh summer
    fruits, such as red and
    white currants, blueberries,
    raspberries, and
    small strawberries

method

1 To make the dough, sift the flour and confectioners' sugar into a bowl. Stir in the ground almonds. Add the butter and rub in until the mixture resembles bread crumbs. Add the egg yolk and milk and work in with a spatula, then mix with your fingers until the dough binds together. Wrap the dough in plastic wrap and let chill in the refrigerator for 30 minutes.

2 On a floured counter, roll out the dough and use to line 12 deep tartlet or individual brioche pans. Prick the bottoms. Press a piece of foil into each tartlet, covering the edges, and bake in a preheated oven, 400°F/200°C, for 10–15 minutes, or until light golden brown. Remove the foil and bake for 2–3 minutes more. Transfer to a wire rack to cool.

3 To make the filling, place the cream cheese and confectioners' sugar in a bowl and mix together. Place a spoonful of filling in each tart shell and arrange the fruit on top. Dust with sifted confectioners' sugar and serve.

full of fruit

In many cultures, the "dessert" usually consists of nothing more than a selection of fresh, seasonal fruit. This, of course, has much to commend it, because all the essential vitamin content of the fruit is preserved when eaten this way—but when there are so many marvelous ways to turn a simple fruit into something a little different and truly delicious, it seems a shame not to experiment!

A great way to start is to take a selection of fresh fruits and serve them with a chocolate fondue—this really is the best of both worlds. In Mediterranean countries, where fruit grows in abundance, it is often poached or baked. The Spiced Apricots in Red Wine from France are very good—the cooking liquid is reduced to a thick, flavorful syrup for pouring over the fruit—as are the Valencia Caramel Oranges from Spain and the Marsala Cherries from Italy. If you love fresh figs, try them broiled with honey and served with a frothy sabayon sauce—sprinkling the figs with a little chopped rosemary as you broil them is optional, but well worth doing.

Exotic fruits are given an unusual twist here. Try serving your favorite encased in a chocolate crèpe, or serve colorful Steamed Spiced Exotic Fruits in their own little "bag." And children will love Toffee Bananas, coated in crisp caramel and irresistible!

broiled honeyed figs with sabayon

ingredients

SERVES 4

8 fresh figs, cut in half

4 tbsp honey

2 fresh rosemary sprigs,
  leaves removed and
  finely chopped (optional)

3 eggs

method

1 Preheat the broiler to high. Arrange the figs, cut-side up, on the broiler pan. Brush with half the honey and sprinkle over the chopped rosemary, if using. Cook under the preheated broiler for 5–6 minutes, or until just starting to caramelize.

2 Meanwhile, to make the sabayon, in a large, heatproof bowl, lightly whisk the eggs with the remaining honey, then place over a pan of simmering water. Using a hand-held electric whisk, beat the eggs and honey together for 10 minutes, or until pale and thick.

3 Put 4 fig halves on each of 4 serving plates, add a generous spoonful of the sabayon, and serve at once.

baked stuffed honey figs

ingredients

SERVES 4

5 fl oz/150 ml/²/₃ cup fresh
    orange juice
6 tbsp honey
12 no-soak dried figs
1¹/₂ oz/40 g shelled pistachio
    nuts, chopped finely
1 oz/25 g no-soak dried
    apricots, chopped very finely
1 tsp sesame seeds
plain yogurt, to serve

method

1 Put the orange juice and 5 tablespoons of the honey in a saucepan and heat gently to dissolve the honey. Add the figs and simmer for 10 minutes or until softened. Remove from the heat and cool in the liquid.

2 Meanwhile, prepare the filling. Put the nuts, apricots, sesame seeds, and remaining tablespoon of honey in a bowl and mix well.

3 Using a slotted spoon, remove the figs from the cooking liquid and reserve. Cut a slit at the top of each fig, where the stem joins. Using your fingers, plump up the figs and stuff each one with about 1 teaspoon of the filling mixture. Close the top of each fig and place in an ovenproof dish. Pour over the reserved cooking liquid.

4 Bake the figs in a preheated oven, 325°F/ 170°C, for 10 minutes or until hot. Serve warm or cold, with the sauce and plain yogurt.

108 full of fruit

grilled bananas

ingredients

SERVES 4

2 oz/55 g block creamed
   coconut, chopped
5 fl oz/150 ml/²/₃ cup
   heavy cream
4 bananas
juice and rind of 1 lime
1 tbsp vegetable or peanut oil
1³/₄ oz/50 g/scant ¹/₂ cup dry
   unsweetened coconut
lime segments, to serve

method

1 Put the creamed coconut and cream in a small pan and heat gently until the coconut has dissolved. Remove from the heat and set aside to cool for 10 minutes, then whisk until thick but floppy.

2 Peel the bananas and toss in the lime juice and rind. Lightly oil a preheated grill pan and cook the bananas, turning once, for 2–3 minutes, until soft and browned.

3 Toast the dry unsweetened coconut on a piece of foil under a broiler until lightly browned. Serve the bananas with lime segments and the coconut cream, sprinkled with the toasted coconut.

toffee bananas

ingredients

SERVES 4

2¹/₂ oz/70 g/¹/₂ cup
   self-rising flour
1 egg, beaten
5 tbsp iced water
4 large, ripe bananas
3 tbsp lemon juice
2 tbsp rice flour
vegetable oil, for deep-frying

caramel

4 oz/115 g/generous ¹/₂ cup
   superfine sugar
4 tbsp iced water, plus an
   extra bowl of iced water
   for setting
2 tbsp sesame seeds

method

1 Sift the flour into a bowl. Make a well in the center, add the egg and the iced water, and beat from the center outwards, until combined into a smooth batter.

2 Peel the bananas and cut into 2-inch/5-cm pieces. Gently shape them into balls with your hands. Brush with lemon juice to prevent discoloration, then roll them in rice flour until coated. Pour oil into a pan to a depth of 2¹/₂ inches/6 cm and preheat to 375°F/190°C. Coat the balls in the batter, and cook in batches in the hot oil for about 2 minutes each, until golden. Lift them out and drain on paper towels.

3 To make the caramel, put the sugar into a small pan over low heat. Add the iced water and heat, stirring, until the sugar dissolves. Simmer for 5 minutes, remove from the heat, and stir in the sesame seeds. Toss the banana balls in the caramel, scoop them out, and drop into the bowl of iced water to set. Lift them out and divide among individual serving bowls. Serve hot.

banana-stuffed crêpes

ingredients

SERVES 4

8 oz/225 g/1½ cups
   all-purpose flour
2 tbsp soft light brown sugar
2 eggs
15 fl oz/450 ml/generous
   1¾ cups milk
grated rind and juice of 1 lemon
2 oz/55 g butter
3 bananas
4 tbsp corn syrup

method

1 Combine the flour and sugar and beat in the eggs and half the milk. Beat together until smooth. Gradually add the remaining milk, stirring constantly to make a smooth batter. Stir in the lemon rind.

2 Melt a little butter in an 8-inch/20-cm skillet and pour in one quarter of the batter. Tilt the skillet to coat the bottom and cook for 1–2 minutes, until set. Flip the crêpe over and cook the second side. Slide out of the skillet and keep warm. Repeat to make 3 more crêpes.

3 Slice the bananas and toss in the lemon juice. Pour the syrup over them and toss together. Fold each crêpe in half and then in half again and fill the center with the banana mixture. Serve warm.

baked stuffed peaches

ingredients

SERVES 4

4 ripe peaches

4 tbsp sweet butter

2 tbsp soft brown sugar

2 oz/55 g/1 cup crushed
amaretti or macaroons

2 tbsp Amaretto liqueur

4 fl oz/125 ml/^{1}/$_2$ cup
light cream, to serve

method

1 Prepare the peaches by cutting them in half and removing the pits (if you want to peel them, just dip them into boiling water for 10–15 seconds and then plunge them into cold water). Place the peaches cut sides up in an ovenproof dish greased with 1 tablespoon of the butter.

2 In a bowl, combine the remaining butter and sugar until creamy, then add the amaretti or macaroons, and mix well. Stuff the peaches with the cookie filling.

3 Bake in the center of a preheated oven, 350°F/180°C, for 20–25 minutes, or until the peaches are soft. Pour over the liqueur and serve hot with the light cream.

peaches with raspberry sauce

ingredients

SERVES 4-6

1 lb/450 g fresh raspberries

finely grated rind of 1 orange

2 tbsp freshly squeezed
    orange juice

2 tbsp Grand Marnier,
    Cointreau, or other
    orange-flavored liqueur

2–3 tbsp superfine sugar

6 ripe fresh peaches

vanilla ice cream, to serve

cats' tongues (optional)

method

1 Purée the raspberries in a food processor or blender, then press through a fine nonmetallic strainer into a mixing bowl to remove the seeds.

2 Stir the orange rind and juice and liqueur into the raspberry purée. Add sugar to taste, stirring until the sugar dissolves. Cover and let chill in the refrigerator until required.

3 Meanwhile, bring a large pan of water to a boil over high heat. Add the peaches, 1 or 2 at a time, and let stand in the water for 10–20 seconds, then remove with a slotted spoon. When the peaches are cool enough to handle, peel off the skins, then cut them in half and remove the pits.

4 Cut each peach half into two and stir into the raspberry sauce. Cover and let chill in the refrigerator until required.

5 When ready to serve, put a scoop or two of ice cream into individual glasses or bowls, then top with the peaches and spoon some extra sauce over. Serve with the cats' tongues on the side, if using.

baked apricots with honey

ingredients

SERVES 4

butter, for greasing

4 apricots, each cut in half
  and pitted

4 tbsp slivered almonds

4 tbsp honey

pinch ground ginger or
  grated nutmeg

vanilla ice cream, to serve
  (optional)

method

1 Lightly butter an ovenproof dish large enough to hold the apricot halves in a single layer.

2 Arrange the apricot halves in the dish, cut sides up. Sprinkle with the almonds and drizzle the honey over. Dust with the spice.

3 Bake in a preheated oven, 400°F/200°C, for 12–15 minutes until the apricots are tender and the almonds golden. Remove from the oven and serve at once, with ice cream on the side, if desired.

spiced apricots in red wine

ingredients

SERVES 4–6

$^1/_2$ tsp white peppercorns,
   lightly crushed

3 cloves

12 fl oz/375 ml/1$^1/_2$ cups
   full-bodied red wine, such
   as Côtes du Rhône

7 fl oz/200 ml/generous
   $^3/_4$ cup water

7 oz/200 g/1 cup sugar

$^1/_2$-inch/1-cm piece of fresh
   gingerroot, peeled
   and finely sliced

1 cinnamon stick

6 tender fresh apricots

freshly grated nutmeg

2 tbsp toasted slivered
   almonds, to decorate

crème fraîche, to serve
   (optional)

method

1 Place the peppercorns and cloves in a dry sauté pan or skillet over high heat and toast, stirring constantly, for 1 minute, or until the aroma develops. Immediately tip them out of the pan. Place the peppercorns in a mortar and lightly crush with a pestle.

2 Put the wine, water, sugar, peppercorns, cloves, gingerroot, and cinnamon stick in a heavy-bottom pan over high heat and stir to dissolve the sugar. When the sugar has dissolved, bring the liquid to a boil, without stirring, and let boil for 8 minutes.

3 Add the apricots to the syrup, then reduce the heat to low and simmer for 5 minutes, or until just tender when pierced with the tip of a knife. Use a slotted spoon to remove the apricots from the syrup and transfer to a bowl of iced water to cool. When the apricots are cool enough to handle, peel them, then cut them in half, remove the pits, and transfer to a serving bowl.

4 Meanwhile, return the syrup to boiling point and boil until it becomes thick. Grate in the nutmeg to taste. Remove the syrup from the heat and let it cool, then pour it over the apricot halves. Cover and let chill.

5 Serve the apricots with a generous portion of the syrup, the toasted slivered almonds, and a dollop of crème fraîche on the side, if using.

oranges in caramel sauce

ingredients

SERVES 6

9 oranges

6 fl oz/175 ml/³/₄ cup water

9 oz/250 g/1¹/₃ cups white
granulated sugar

3 tbsp Greek honey

method

1 Using a zester, remove the zest from the oranges and put in a small pan. Add the water and leave to soak for 1 hour.

2 When the orange zest has soaked, simmer for 20 minutes. Strain any remaining liquid, reserving the zest, into a measuring cup and add water to make 6 fl oz/175 ml/3/4 cup.

3 Using a sharp knife, remove the peel from the oranges, discarding all the white pith. Cut the flesh widthwise into ¹/₄-inch/5-mm slices and arrange in a glass serving dish, scattered with a little of the orange zest. Reserve most of the zest to decorate.

4 Put the measured orange water and the sugar in a pan and heat until the sugar has dissolved, then bring to a boil and boil rapidly until it turns a pale golden color. Immediately remove from the heat, stir in the honey until dissolved, and then add the reserved orange zest. Let cool slightly, then pour the caramel sauce over the oranges. Chill in the refrigerator for at least 3 hours before serving, decorated with the reserved zest.

valencia caramel oranges

ingredients

SERVES 4–6

4 large, juicy oranges

9 oz/250 g/generous
   1¼ cups superfine sugar

10 fl oz/300 ml/
   1¼ cups water

4–6 tbsp slivered almonds,
   toasted, to serve

sprig of fresh mint, to garnish

method

1 Working over a heatproof bowl to catch any juices, and using a small serrated knife, pare the oranges, taking care not to leave any of the bitter-tasting pith. Use the knife to remove the orange segments, cutting between the membranes. Squeeze the empty membranes over the bowl to extract as much juice as possible; discard the membranes and set the segments and juice aside.

2 Put the sugar and 5 fl oz/150 ml/⅔ cup of the water into a small, heavy-bottom pan over medium-high heat. Stir until the sugar dissolves, then bring to a boil and boil, without stirring, until the syrup turns a rich golden brown.

3 Pour the remaining water into the pan (stand back because the caramel will splatter). Stir again until the caramel dissolves. Remove from the heat and let the caramel cool slightly, then pour over the oranges. Stir to blend the orange juice into the caramel. Let the oranges cool completely, then cover with plastic wrap and let chill for at least 2 hours before serving.

4 Just before serving, sprinkle the caramel oranges with the toasted slivered almonds. Garnish with a sprig of fresh mint.

roasted spicy pineapple

ingredients

SERVES 4

1 pineapple

1 mango, peeled, seeded,
    and sliced

2 oz/55 g butter

4 tbsp corn syrup

1–2 tsp cinnamon

1 tsp freshly grated nutmeg

4 tbsp soft brown sugar

2 passion fruit

5 fl oz/150 ml/^{2}/$_3$ cup
    sour cream

finely grated rind of 1 orange

method

1 Use a sharp knife to cut off the top, base, and skin of the pineapple, then cut into quarters. Remove the central core and cut the flesh into large cubes. Place them in a roasting pan with the mango.

2 Place the butter, syrup, cinnamon, nutmeg, and sugar in a small pan and heat gently, stirring constantly, until melted. Pour the mixture over the fruit. Roast in a preheated oven, 400°F/200°C, for 20–30 minutes, until the fruit is browned.

3 Halve the passion fruit and scoop out the seeds. Spoon over the roasted fruit. Mix the sour cream and orange rind together and serve with the fruit.

pears in honey syrup

ingredients

SERVES 4

4 medium-ripe pears

7 fl oz/200 ml/generous
   $^3/_4$ cup water

1 tsp sugar

1 tbsp honey

method

1 Peel each pear, leaving the stem intact. Wrap each in foil and place in a pan with the stems resting on the side of the pan. Add enough water to cover at least half of the height of the pears. Bring to a boil and simmer for 30 minutes. Remove the pears and carefully remove the foil, reserving any juices. Set aside to cool.

2 Bring the measured water to a boil. Add any pear juices, the sugar, and honey and boil for 5 minutes. Remove from the heat and let cool a little.

3 Place each pear in an individual dish. Pour a little syrup over each and serve just warm.

poached pears with chocolate sauce

ingredients

SERVES 4

4 ripe dessert pears, such as
  Conference
juice of $^1/_2$ lemon
12 fl oz/325 ml/1$^1/_2$ cups
  Beaumes-de-Venise
  dessert wine
6 fl oz/175 ml/$^3/_4$ cup water
1 vanilla bean, split
vanilla ice cream, to serve

chocolate sauce

6 oz/175 g bittersweet
  chocolate, broken up
5 tbsp water
4 tbsp heavy cream

method

1 Peel and core the pears, then cut into quarters, dropping them into a bowl of water with the lemon juice squeezed in to prevent discoloration.

2 Put the wine, water, and split vanilla bean in a sauté pan over high heat. Add the pear quarters and bring the liquid to a boil. As soon as it boils, reduce the heat to the point where small bubbles appear around the edge. Poach the pears for 5–10 minutes or until they are tender when pierced with the tip of a knife.

3 Use a slotted spoon to transfer the pear quarters to an ovenproof serving dish as they become tender. When all the pears are removed from the liquid, return the liquid to a boil and continue boiling until reduced to about 4 tablespoons. Pour the syrup and vanilla bean over the pears and let cool completely. Cover the surface with plastic wrap and chill for at least 1 hour or overnight.

4 Just before serving, make the chocolate sauce. Stir the chocolate and water in a small pan over low heat until melted and smooth. Remove from the heat and beat in the cream.

5 To serve, spoon a scoop of ice cream into individual serving bowls and add the poached pears. Spoon over the hot chocolate sauce.

marsala cherries

ingredients

SERVES 4

5 oz/140 g/⅝ cup
  superfine sugar
thinly pared rind of 1 lemon
2-in/5-cm piece of cinnamon
  stick
8 fl oz/250 ml/1 cup water
8 fl oz/250 ml/1 cup Marsala
2 lb/900 g Morello cherries,
  pitted
5 fl oz/150 ml/⅔ cup
  heavy cream

method

1 Put the sugar, lemon rind, cinnamon stick, water, and Marsala in a heavy-bottom pan and bring to a boil, stirring constantly. Reduce the heat and let simmer for 5 minutes. Remove the cinnamon stick.

2 Add the Morello cherries, cover, and let simmer gently for 10 minutes. Using a slotted spoon, transfer the cherries to a bowl.

3 Return the pan to the heat and bring to a boil over high heat. Boil for 3–4 minutes, until thick and syrupy. Pour the syrup over the cherries and set aside to cool, then chill for at least 1 hour.

4 Whip the cream until stiff peaks form. To serve, divide the cherries and syrup among 4 individual dishes or glasses and top with the whipped cream.

poached fruit, seville style

ingredients

SERVES 4–6

1/2 tsp fennel seeds

1/2 tsp coriander seeds

1/4 tsp black peppercorns

7 oz/200 g/1 cup
   superfine sugar

8 fl oz/250 ml/1 cup
   red wine, such as Rioja

8 fl oz/250 ml/1 cup water

3 tbsp freshly squeezed
   orange juice

2 tbsp freshly squeezed
   lemon juice

2 tbsp Spanish cream sherry

3 cloves

1 cinnamon stick

12 tender apricots, halved
   and pitted

2 tbsp slivered almonds,
   toasted, to decorate

method

1 To make the red wine syrup, put the fennel seeds, coriander seeds, and peppercorns in a heavy-bottom pan over high heat and dry-fry for up to about 1 minute until they start to give off an aroma. Immediately tip them out of the pan to stop the cooking. Put in a mortar and lightly crush.

2 Put the sugar, wine, water, orange and lemon juices, sherry, and all the spices into a heavy-bottom pan over medium-high heat, stirring to dissolve the sugar. Bring to a boil, without stirring, and let bubble for 5 minutes. Add the fruit and let simmer for 6–8 minutes until tender. Remove the pan from the heat, transfer to a bowl of iced water, and let cool. When cool enough to handle, remove the apricots, and peel. Cover and let chill until required.

3 Meanwhile, return the juices to the heat and boil until the syrup thickens and the flavors become more concentrated. Remove from the heat and let cool.

4 To serve, place the fruit in serving bowls, spoon the syrup over, then sprinkle with slivered almonds.

warm fruit nests

ingredients

SERVES 4

2–3 tbsp lemon-infused
    olive oil

8 sheets of frozen filo
    pastry, thawed

9 oz/250 g blueberries

9 oz/250 g raspberries

9 oz/250 g blackberries

3 tbsp superfine sugar

1 tsp ground allspice

sprigs of fresh mint,
    to decorate

heavy cream, to serve

method

1 Brush 4 small muffin pans with oil. Cut the filo pastry into 16 squares measuring about 12 cm/4^1/$_2$ inches across. Brush each square with oil and use to line the muffin pans. Place 4 sheets in each pan, staggering them so that the overhanging corners make a decorative star shape. Transfer to a cookie sheet and bake in a preheated oven, 350°F/ 180°C, for 7–8 minutes, until golden. Remove from the oven and set aside.

2 Meanwhile, warm the fruit in a pan with the superfine sugar and allspice over medium heat until simmering. Lower the heat and continue simmering, stirring, for 10 minutes. Remove from the heat and drain. Using a perforated spoon, divide the warm fruit among the tartlet shells. Garnish with sprigs of fresh mint and serve warm with heavy cream.

mixed fruit salad

ingredients

SERVES 4

1 papaya, halved, peeled,
   and seeded

2 bananas, sliced thickly

1 small pineapple, peeled,
   halved, cored, and sliced

12 lychees, peeled if fresh

1 small melon, halved,
   peeled, seeded, and cut
   into thin wedges

2 oranges

grated rind and juice of 1 lime

2 tbsp superfine sugar

method

1 Arrange the papaya, bananas, pineapple, lychees, and melon on a serving platter. Cut off the rind and pith from the oranges. Cut the orange segments out from between the membranes and add to the fruit platter. Grate a small quantity of the discarded orange rind and add to the platter.

2 Combine the lime rind, juice, and sugar. Pour over the salad and serve.

steamed spiced exotic fruits

ingredients

SERVES 4

2 kiwi fruit, peeled and halved

4 rambutan or lychees,
    peeled, halved, and
    stoned

2 passion fruit, the flesh
    scooped out

8 Cape gooseberries
    (physalis), papery leaves
    removed and fruit halved

3 oz/85 g mango, cut into
    $^3/_4$-inch/2-cm cubes

1 sharon fruit, cut into
    $^3/_4$-inch/2-cm slices

3 oz/85 g fresh raspberries

2 vanilla beans, split in half
    lengthwise

2 cinnamon sticks,
    broken in half

4 star anise

4 fresh bay leaves

4 tbsp freshly squeezed
    orange juice

method

1 Cut four 16 x 16-inch/40 x 40-cm squares of parchment paper and four foil squares of the same size. Put each parchment paper square on top of a foil square and fold diagonally in half to form a triangle. Open up.

2 Divide the fruits into 4 and arrange each portion neatly in the center of each opened square. Add a vanilla bean half, a cinnamon stick half, a star anise, a bay leaf, and 1 tablespoon of orange juice to each triangle.

3 Close each triangle over the mixture, fold in the corners, and crumple the edges together to form airtight triangular bags. Transfer the bags to a cookie sheet and bake in a preheated oven, 400°F/200°C, for 10–12 minutes, or until they puff up with steam.

4 To serve, put each bag on a serving plate and snip open at the table.

chocolate fondue

ingredients

SERVES 6

1 pineapple

1 mango

12 cape gooseberries

9 oz/250 g/generous 1 cup
  fresh strawberries

9 oz/250 g/generous
  1¹/₂ cups seeded
  green grapes

fondue

9 oz/250 g semisweet
  chocolate,
  broken into pieces

5 fl oz/150 ml/²/₃ cup
  heavy cream

2 tbsp brandy

method

1 Using a sharp knife, peel and core the pineapple, then cut the flesh into cubes. Peel the mango and cut the flesh into cubes. Peel back the papery outer skin of the cape gooseberries and twist at the top to make a "handle." Arrange all the fruit on 6 serving plates and let chill in the refrigerator.

2 To make the fondue, place the chocolate and cream in a fondue pot. Heat gently, stirring constantly, until the chocolate has melted. Stir in the brandy until thoroughly blended and the chocolate mixture is smooth.

3 Place the fondue pot over the burner to keep warm. To serve, allow each guest to dip the fruit into the sauce, using fondue forks or bamboo skewers.

exotic fruit chocolate crêpes

ingredients

SERVES 4

3¹/₂ oz/100 g/³/₄ cup
    all-purpose flour
2 tbsp unsweetened cocoa
pinch of salt
1 egg, beaten
10 fl oz/300 ml/1¹/₄ cups milk
oil, for frying
confectioners' sugar,
    for dusting

filling

3¹/₂ oz/100 g/scant ¹/₂ cup
    strained plain yogurt
9 oz/250 g/1¹/₈ cups
    Mascarpone cheese
confectioners' sugar (optional)
1 mango, peeled and diced
8 oz/225 g/generous 1 cup
    strawberries, hulled
    and quartered
2 passion fruit

method

1 To make the filling, place the yogurt and Mascarpone cheese in a bowl and sweeten with confectioners' sugar, if you like. Place the mango and strawberries in a bowl and mix together. Cut the passion fruit in half, scoop out the pulp and seeds, and add to the mango and strawberries. Stir together, then set aside.

2 To make the crêpes, sift the flour, unsweetened cocoa, and salt into a bowl and make a well in the center. Add the egg and whisk with a balloon whisk. Gradually beat in the milk, drawing in the flour from the sides, to make a smooth batter. Cover and let stand for 20 minutes. Heat a small amount of oil in a 7-inch/18-cm crêpe pan or skillet. Pour in just enough batter to thinly coat the bottom of the pan. Cook over medium-high heat for 1 minute, then turn and cook the other side for 30–60 seconds, or until cooked through.

3 Transfer the crêpe to a plate and keep hot. Repeat with the remaining batter, stacking the cooked crêpes on top of each other with parchment paper in between. Keep warm in the oven while cooking the remainder. To serve, divide the filling among the crêpes, then roll up and dust with confectioners' sugar.

pavlova

ingredients

SERVES 4

6 egg whites

pinch of cream of tartar

pinch of salt

9³/₄ oz/275 g/1¹/₂ cups superfine sugar

20 fl oz/625 ml/2¹/₂ cups heavy cream

1 tsp vanilla essence

2 kiwi fruits, peeled and sliced

9 oz/250 g strawberries, hulled and sliced

3 ripe peaches, sliced

1 ripe mango, peeled and sliced

2 tbsp orange liqueur, such as Cointreau

fresh mint leaves, to decorate

method

1 Line 3 baking sheets with parchment paper, then draw an 8¹/₂-inch/22-cm circle in the center of each one. Beat the egg whites into stiff peaks. Mix in the cream of tartar and salt. Gradually add 7 oz/200 g/⁷/₈ cup of the sugar. Beat for 2 minutes until glossy. Fill a piping bag with the meringue mixture and pipe enough to fill each circle, doming them slightly in the center. Bake in a preheated oven, 225°F/110°C, for 3 hours. Remove from the oven and let cool.

2 Whip together the cream and vanilla essence with the remaining sugar. Put the fruit into a separate bowl and stir in the liqueur. Put one meringue circle onto a plate, then spread over one-third of the sugared cream. Spread over one-third of the fruit, then top with a meringue circle. Spread over another third of cream, then another third of fruit. Top with the last meringue circle. Spread over the remaining cream, followed by the rest of the fruit. Decorate with mint leaves and serve.

chilled & semi-frozen
desserts

Chilled desserts are the perfect choice for a dinner party, because you make them in advance and then forget about them until it is time to serve them, cool and delicious, to your guests.

For a family meal or a midweek get-together, Creamy Mango Brûlée is a quick version of the classic French dish. If you have more time to spare, and want to impress with a really sophisticated dessert, go for the real thing—Espresso Crème Brûlée, or the Spanish version, Catalan Burned Cream.

An intriguing dish is Floating Islands—poached meringues "floating" in a lake of vanilla sauce and drizzled with caramel. The Zabaglione and Cassata recipes are served "semifreddo," meaning "semi-frozen"—halfway between a chilled dessert and an ice cream, they are enticingly soft and melting.

Tiramisù is a "modern classic" and there are two recipes here, one with a new twist—the coffee-soaked sponge and creamy Mascarpone cheese are layered with fresh cherries. Mascarpone has a natural sweetness, perfect for desserts—try Mascarpone Creams, made with crushed amaretti cookies for a crunchy texture, or Chocolate Brandy Torte, definitely one for the grown-ups! And talking of brandy, try the Zucotto—you make it the day before serving and it's divine!

espresso crème brûlée

ingredients

MAKES 4

16 fl oz/450 ml/scant 2 cups
  heavy cream
1 tbsp instant espresso
  powder
4 large egg yolks
3^1/$_2$ oz/100 g/^{1}/$_2$ cup
  superfine sugar, plus extra
  for glazing
2 tbsp coffee liqueur, such
  as Kahlùa

method

1 Place the cream in a small pan over medium-high heat and heat until small bubbles appear around the edges. Mix in the espresso powder, stirring until it dissolves, then remove the pan from the heat and let stand until completely cool.

2 Lightly beat the egg yolks in a bowl, then add the sugar and continue beating until thick and creamy. Reheat the cream over medium-high heat until small bubbles appear around the edges. Stir into the egg-yolk mixture, beating constantly. Stir in the coffee liqueur.

3 Divide the mixture among 4 shallow porcelain dishes placed on a baking sheet. Bake in a preheated oven, 225°F/110°C, for 35–40 minutes, or until the mixture is just "trembling" when you shake the dishes.

4 Remove from the oven and let cool completely. Cover the surfaces with plastic wrap and let chill in the refrigerator for at least 4 hours, but ideally overnight.

5 Just before you are ready to serve, sprinkle the surface of each dessert with 1 tablespoonful of sugar and caramelize with a kitchen blow-torch or put the dishes under a very hot preheated broiler until the topping is golden and bubbling. Let cool for a few minutes for the caramel to harden before serving.

catalan burned cream

ingredients

SERVES 6

24 fl oz/750 ml/3 cups
 whole milk

1 vanilla bean, split

thinly pared rind of 1/2 lemon

7 large egg yolks

7 oz/200 g/1 cup
 superfine sugar

3 tbsp cornstarch

method

1 A day in advance of serving, pour the milk into a pan with the vanilla bean and lemon rind. Bring to a boil, then remove from the heat and let stand for 30 minutes to infuse.

2 Put the egg yolks and half of the sugar in a heatproof bowl that will fit over a pan without touching the bottom, and beat until the sugar dissolves and the mixture is creamy.

3 Return the infused milk to the heat and bring to a simmer, then stir 4 tablespoons into the cornstarch in a bowl until a smooth paste forms. Stir into the milk over medium-low heat for 1 minute. Strain the milk into the egg mixture and whisk until well blended.

4 Put the bowl over a pan of simmering water and stir the mixture for 25–30 minutes until thick enough to coat the back of the spoon; the bowl must not touch the water or the eggs might scramble. Spoon the mixture into six 4-inch/10-cm round cazuelas or shallow crème brûlée dishes. Let cool completely, then cover and let chill for at least 12 hours.

5 To serve, sprinkle the top of each with a thin layer of superfine sugar. Use a kitchen blowtorch to caramelize the sugar. Let stand while the caramel hardens, then serve. The caramel will remain firm for about 1 hour at room temperature; do not return to the fridge or the caramel will "melt."

creamy mango brûlée

ingredients

SERVES 4

2 mangoes

9 oz/250 g/generous 1 cup
  Mascarpone cheese

7 fl oz/200 ml/generous
  3/4 cup strained
  plain yogurt

1 tsp ground ginger

grated rind and juice of 1 lime

2 tbsp light brown sugar

8 tbsp raw brown sugar

method

1 Slice the mangoes on either side of the seed. Discard the pit and peel the fruit. Slice and then chop the fruit and divide it among 4 ramekins.

2 Beat the Mascarpone cheese with the yogurt. Fold in the ginger, lime rind and juice, and light brown sugar. Divide the mixture among the ramekins and level off the tops. Chill for 2 hours.

3 Sprinkle 2 tablespoons of raw brown sugar over the top of each dish, covering the creamy mixture. Place under a hot broiler for 2–3 minutes, until melted and browned. Let cool, then chill.

spanish caramel flan

ingredients

SERVES 6

18 fl oz/500 ml/scant
   2$^{1}/_{2}$ cups whole milk
$^{1}/_{2}$ orange with 2 long, thin
   pieces of rind removed
1 vanilla bean, split, or
   $^{1}/_{2}$ tsp vanilla extract
6 oz/175 g/scant 1 cup
   superfine sugar
butter, for greasing the dish
3 large eggs, plus 2 large
   egg yolks

method

1 Pour the milk into a pan with the orange rind and vanilla bean or extract. Bring to a boil, then remove from the heat and stir in half of the sugar; set aside for at least 30 minutes to infuse.

2 Meanwhile, put the remaining sugar and 4 tablespoons of water in another pan over medium-high heat. Stir until the sugar dissolves, then boil without stirring until the caramel turns deep golden brown. Immediately remove the pan from the heat and squeeze in a few drops of orange juice to stop the cooking. Pour into a lightly buttered 1$^{1}/_{2}$-pint/1-liter/5-cup soufflé dish and swirl to cover the base; set aside.

3 Return the pan of infused milk to the heat, and bring to a simmer. Beat the whole eggs and egg yolks together in a heatproof bowl. Pour the warm milk into the eggs, whisking constantly. Strain into the soufflé dish.

4 Place the soufflé dish in a roasting pan and pour in enough boiling water to come halfway up the sides of the dish. Bake in a preheated oven, 325°F/160°C, for 75–90 minutes until set and a knife inserted in the center comes out clean. Remove the soufflé dish from the roasting pan and set aside to cool completely. Cover and let chill overnight. To serve, run a metal spatula round the soufflé, then invert onto a serving plate, shaking firmly to release.

floating islands

ingredients

SERVES 4–6

32 fl oz/1 liter/4 cups milk, plus a little extra if necessary to make up the vanilla sauce

1 vanilla bean, split

5½ oz/150 g/¾ cup superfine sugar

6 egg yolks

1½ tbsp water

squeeze of lemon juice

meringues

2 large egg whites

½ tsp cream of tartar

2 oz/55 g/scant ⅓ cup superfine sugar

2 oz/55 g/½ cup confectioners' sugar

method

1 To make the meringues, whisk the egg whites until frothy. Beat in the cream of tartar, and continue whisking until soft peaks form. Adding the superfine sugar 1 tablespoon at a time, whisk until stiff peaks form. Sift over the confectioners' sugar and beat until glossy.

2 Slowly bring the milk to a boil over medium-high heat in a wide skillet, then reduce the heat. Using a large spoon dipped in water, drop one quarter of the meringue mixture into the simmering milk. Poach for 5 minutes, then let drain on a dish towel. Make 4 meringues.

3 Strain the milk and measure 20 fl oz/625 ml/ 2½ cups. Add the vanilla bean and bring to a boil in a pan over medium heat. Remove from the heat, cover, and let stand. Beat 3½ oz/ 100 g/½ cup of the sugar in a bowl with the egg yolks until thick and creamy. Remove the vanilla bean, then pour one quarter of the milk into the egg mixture, beating constantly. Return to the pan and simmer, stirring, for 10 minutes. Let cool, then pour into 4 bowls. Add the meringues. Cover and let chill.

4 Just before serving, dissolve the remaining sugar, stirring, in the water over medium-high heat. Bring to a boil, without stirring, and let bubble until a dark golden brown. Remove from the heat and add the lemon juice. To serve, drizzle the caramel over the meringues.

creamy chocolate dessert

ingredients

SERVES 4–6

6 oz/175 g semisweet
    chocolate, at least 70%
    cocoa solids, broken up
1¹/₂ tbsp orange juice
3 tbsp water
2 tbsp unsalted butter, diced
2 eggs, separated
¹/₈ tsp cream of tartar
3 tbsp superfine sugar
6 tbsp heavy cream
orange wedges, to garnish

pistachio-orange praline
2 oz/55 g/generous ¹/₄ cup
    superfine sugar
2 oz/55 g/scant ¹/₂ cup
    shelled pistachios
corn oil, for greasing
finely grated rind of 1 large
    orange

method

1 Melt the chocolate with the orange juice and water in a pan over very low heat, stirring constantly. Remove from the heat and stir in the butter until melted. Using a rubber spatula, scrape the chocolate into a bowl.

2 Beat the egg yolks until blended, then beat them into the chocolate mixture. Let cool.

3 In a clean bowl, whisk the egg whites with the cream of tartar until soft peaks form. Add the sugar, 1 tablespoon at a time, beating well after each addition, until the meringue is glossy. Beat 1 tablespoon of the meringue into the chocolate mixture, then fold in the rest.

4 In a separate bowl, whip the cream until soft peaks form. Fold into the chocolate mixture. Spoon into individual glass bowls, cover with plastic wrap, and let chill for at least 4 hours.

5 Meanwhile, to make the praline, put the sugar and pistachios in a pan over medium heat. When the sugar starts to melt, stir gently until a liquid caramel forms and the nuts start popping. Pour onto a baking sheet lightly greased with corn oil and finely grate the orange rind over. Let cool until firm then coarsely chop. Just before serving, sprinkle the praline over the chocolate dessert. Garnish with orange wedges.

coffee panna cotta with chocolate sauce

ingredients

SERVES 6

oil, for brushing

20 fl oz/600 ml/$2^1/_2$ cups heavy cream

1 vanilla pod

2 oz/55 g/$^1/_3$ cup golden superfine sugar

2 tsp instant espresso coffee granules, dissolved in 4 tbsp water

2 tsp powdered gelatin

chocolate-covered coffee beans, to serve

unsweetened cocoa powder, to serve

chocolate sauce

5 fl oz/150 ml/$^2/_3$ cup light cream

2 oz/55 g semisweet chocolate, melted

method

1 Lightly brush 6 x 5-fl oz /150-ml/$^2/_3$-cup molds with oil. Place the cream in a pan. Split the vanilla bean and scrape the black seeds into the cream. Add the vanilla bean and the sugar, then heat gently until almost boiling. Strain the cream into a heatproof bowl and set aside. Place the coffee in a small heatproof bowl, sprinkle on the gelatin and let stand for 5 minutes, or until spongy. Set the bowl over a pan of gently simmering water until the gelatin has dissolved.

2 Stir a little of the reserved cream into the gelatin mixture, then stir the gelatin mixture into the remainder of the cream. Divide the mixture among the prepared molds and let cool, then let chill in the refrigerator for 8 hours, or overnight.

3 To make the sauce, place one-quarter of the cream in a bowl and stir in the melted chocolate. Gradually stir in the remaining cream, reserving 1 tablespoon. To serve the panna cotta, dip the base of the molds briefly into hot water and turn out onto 6 dessert plates. Pour the chocolate cream round. Dot drops of the reserved cream onto the sauce and feather it with a toothpick. Decorate with chocolate-covered coffee beans and dust with unsweetened cocoa powder to serve.

chocolate coeurs à la crème

ingredients

SERVES 8

8 oz/225 g/generous 1 cup
   ricotta cheese
2 oz/55 g/$^1/_2$ cup
   confectioners'
   sugar, sifted
10 fl oz/300 ml/1$^1/_4$ cups
   heavy cream
1 tsp vanilla extract
2 oz/55 g semisweet
   chocolate, grated
2 egg whites

coulis

8 oz/225 g/1 cup fresh
   raspberries
confectioners' sugar, to taste

to decorate

fresh strawberries, halved
fresh raspberries

method

1 Line 8 individual molds with cheesecloth. Press the ricotta cheese through a strainer into a bowl. Add the confectioners' sugar, cream, and vanilla extract and beat together thoroughly. Stir in the grated chocolate. Place the egg whites in a separate clean bowl and whisk until stiff but not dry. Gently fold into the cheese mixture.

2 Spoon the mixture into the prepared molds. Stand the molds on a tray or dish and let drain in the refrigerator for 8 hours, or overnight—the cheesecloth will absorb most of the liquid.

3 To make the raspberry coulis, place the raspberries in a food processor and process to a purée. Press the purée through a strainer into a bowl and add confectioners' sugar, to taste. To serve, turn each dessert out onto a serving plate and pour the raspberry coulis round. Decorate with strawberries and raspberries, then serve.

mascarpone creams

ingredients

SERVES 4

4 oz/115 g Amaretti cookies,
   crushed

4 tbsp Amaretto or Maraschino

4 eggs, separated

2 oz/55 g/generous $1/2$ cup
   superfine sugar

8 oz/225 g/1 cup
   Mascarpone cheese

toasted slivered almonds,
   to decorate

method

1 Place the Amaretti crumbs in a bowl, add the Amaretto or Maraschino, and let soak.

2 Meanwhile, beat the egg yolks with the superfine sugar until pale and thick. Fold in the Mascarpone and soaked cookie crumbs.

3 Whisk the egg whites in a separate, spotlessly clean bowl until stiff, then gently fold into the cheese mixture. Divide the Mascarpone cream among 4 serving dishes and let chill for 1–2 hours. Sprinkle with toasted slivered almonds just before serving.

zabaglione

ingredients

SERVES 4–6

4 egg yolks

$3^1/_2$ oz/100 g/$^1/_2$ cup
superfine sugar

4 fl oz/125 ml/$^1/_2$ cup dry
Marsala

7 fl oz/225 ml/scant 1 cup
heavy whipping cream

shortbread cookies, to serve

method

1 Put the egg yolks and sugar in a large heatproof bowl and whisk together until pale and the mixture leaves a trail when the whisk is lifted. Whisk in the Marsala, a tablespoon at a time, until well blended.

2 Place the bowl over a pan of simmering water and heat gently, whisking all the time, until the mixture has doubled in size. Remove the bowl from the heat, stand the bowl in cold water, and whisk until the mixture is cool.

3 Whip the cream until it holds its shape. Add the whipped cream to the egg mixture, then fold in until well blended.

4 Freeze the mixture in a freezerproof container, uncovered, for 2–3 hours, or until firm or required. Cover the container with a lid for storing.

5 Serve in wine glasses, accompanied by shortbread cookies.

chocolate rum creams

ingredients

SERVES 6

3^1/$_2$ oz/100 g semisweet
   chocolate, broken
   into pieces

5 fl oz/150 ml/^{2}/$_3$ cup
   light cream

10 fl oz/300 ml/1^1/$_4$ cups
   whipping cream

1 tbsp confectioners'
   sugar, sifted

2 tbsp white rum

chocolate curls, to decorate

method

1 Place the chocolate and light cream in a small, heavy-bottom pan and heat very gently until the chocolate has melted. Stir until smooth, then remove from the heat and let cool. Pour the whipping cream into a large bowl and, using an electric whisk, whip until thick but not stiff.

2 Carefully whisk the sugar, rum, and cooled chocolate mixture into the whipped cream. Take care not to overwhisk.

3 Spoon the mixture into 6 serving dishes or glasses, cover with plastic wrap, and let chill in the refrigerator for 1–2 hours. Sprinkle chocolate curls carefully over the creams before serving.

chocolate mousse

ingredients

SERVES 4–6

8 oz/225 g bittersweet
  chocolate, chopped

2 tbsp brandy, Grand Marnier,
  or Cointreau

4 tbsp water

1 oz/30 g unsalted
  butter, diced

3 large eggs, separated

1/4 tsp cream of tartar

2 oz/55 g/1/4 cup sugar

4 fl oz/125 ml/1/2 cup
  heavy cream

method

1 Place the chocolate, brandy, and water in a small pan over low heat and melt, stirring, until smooth. Remove the pan from the heat and beat in the butter. Beat the egg yolks into the chocolate mixture, one after another, until blended, then let cool slightly.

2 Meanwhile, using an electric mixer on low speed, beat the egg whites in a spotlessly clean bowl until frothy, then gradually increase the mixer's speed and beat until soft peaks form. Sprinkle the cream of tartar over the surface, then add the sugar, tablespoon by tablespoon, and continue beating until stiff peaks form. Beat several tablespoons of the egg whites into the chocolate mixture to loosen.

3 In another bowl, whip the cream until soft peaks form. Spoon the cream over the chocolate mixture, then spoon the remaining whites over the cream. Use a large metal spoon or rubber spatula to fold the chocolate into the cream and egg whites.

4 Either spoon the chocolate mousse into a large serving bowl or divide among 4 or 6 individual bowls. Cover the bowl(s) with plastic wrap and chill the mousse for at least 3 hours before serving.

white chocolate mousse

ingredients

SERVES 6

9 oz/250 g white chocolate,
   broken into pieces

3^1/$_2$ fl oz/100 ml/generous
   ^{1}/$_3$ cup milk

10 fl oz/300 ml/1^1/$_4$ cups
   heavy cream

1 tsp rose water

2 egg whites

4 oz/115 g semisweet
   chocolate, broken
   into pieces

candied rose petals,
   to decorate

method

1 Place the white chocolate and milk in a pan and heat gently until the chocolate has melted, then stir. Transfer to a large bowl and let cool.

2 Whip the cream and rose water in a separate bowl until soft peaks form. Whisk the egg whites in a separate large, spotlessly clean, greasefree bowl until stiff but not dry. Gently fold the whipped cream into the white chocolate mixture, then fold in the egg whites. Spoon the mixture into 6 small dishes or glasses, cover with plastic wrap and let chill for 8 hours, or overnight, to set.

3 Melt the semisweet chocolate and let cool, then pour evenly over the mousses. Let stand until the chocolate has hardened, then decorate with rose petals and serve.

chestnut & chocolate terrine

ingredients

SERVES 6

7 fl oz/200 ml/generous
$^3/_4$ cup heavy cream

4 oz/115 g semisweet
chocolate, melted
and cooled

$3^1/_2$ fl oz/100 ml/generous
$^1/_3$ cup rum

1 package rectangular, plain,
sweet cookies

8 oz/225 g canned sweetened
chestnut purée

unsweetened cocoa,
for dusting

confectioners' sugar,
to decorate

method

1 Line a 1-lb/450-g loaf pan with plastic wrap. Place the cream in a bowl and whip lightly until soft peaks form. Using a spatula, fold in the cooled chocolate.

2 Place the rum in a shallow dish. Lightly dip 4 cookies into the rum and arrange on the bottom of the pan. Repeat with 4 more cookies. Spread half the chocolate cream over the cookies. Make another layer of 8 cookies dipped in rum and spread over the chestnut purée, followed by another layer of cookies. Spread over the remaining chocolate cream and top with a final layer of cookies. Cover with plastic wrap and let chill for 8 hours, or preferably overnight.

3 Turn the terrine out on to a large serving dish. Dust with unsweetened cocoa. Cut strips of paper and place these randomly on top of the terrine. Sift over confectioners' sugar. Carefully remove the paper. To serve, dip a sharp knife in hot water, dry it, and use it to cut the terrine into slices.

zucotto

ingredients

SERVES 6

4 oz/115 g soft margarine,
   plus extra for greasing
3^1/$_2$ oz/100 g/scant ^{2}/$_3$ cup
   self-rising flour
2 tbsp unsweetened cocoa
^{1}/$_2$ tsp baking powder
4 oz/115 g/generous ^{1}/$_2$ cup
   golden superfine sugar
2 eggs, beaten
3 tbsp brandy
2 tbsp Kirsch

filling

10 fl oz/300 ml/1^1/$_4$ cups
   heavy cream
1 oz/25 g/^{1}/$_4$ cup
   confectioners' sugar, sifted
2 oz/55 g/^{1}/$_4$ cup toasted
   almonds, chopped
8 oz/225 g black cherries,
   pitted
2 oz/55 g semisweet chocolate,
   finely chopped

to decorate

1 tbsp unsweetened cocoa
1 tbsp confectioners' sugar
fresh cherries

method

1 Grease a 12 x 9-inch/30 x 23-cm jelly roll pan with margarine and line with parchment paper. Sift the flour, cocoa, and baking powder into a bowl. Add the sugar, margarine, and eggs. Beat together until well mixed, then spoon into the prepared pan. Bake in a preheated oven, 375°F/190°C, for 15–20 minutes, or until well risen and firm to the touch. Let stand in the pan for 5 minutes, then turn out onto a wire rack to cool.

2 Using the rim of a 2^1/$_2$-pint/1.2-liter/5-cup ovenproof bowl as a guide, cut a circle from the cake and set aside. Line the bowl with plastic wrap. Use the remaining cake, cutting it as necessary, to line the bowl. Place the brandy and Kirsch in a small bowl and mix together. Sprinkle over the cake, including the reserved circle.

3 To make the filling, pour the cream into a separate bowl and add the confectioners' sugar. Whip until thick, then fold in the almonds, cherries, and chocolate. Fill the sponge mold with the cream mixture and press the cake circle on top. Cover with a plate and a weight, and let chill in the refrigerator for 6–8 hours, or overnight. When ready to serve, turn the zucotto out onto a serving plate. Decorate with cocoa and confectioners' sugar, sifted over in alternating segments, and a few cherries.

chilled chocolate dessert

ingredients

SERVES 4–6

8 oz/225 g/1 cup Mascarpone cheese

2 tbsp finely ground coffee beans

1 oz/25 g/$\frac{1}{4}$ cup confectioners' sugar

3 oz/85 g unsweetened chocolate, grated finely

10 fl oz/300 ml/1$\frac{1}{4}$ cups heavy cream, plus extra to decorate

Marsala, to serve

method

1 Beat the Mascarpone with the coffee and confectioners' sugar until thoroughly combined.

2 Set aside 4 teaspoons of the grated chocolate and stir the remainder into the cheese mixture with 5 tablespoons of the unwhipped cream.

3 Whip the remaining cream until it forms soft peaks. Stir 1 tablespoon of the Mascarpone mixture into the cream to slacken it, then fold the cream into the remaining Mascarpone mixture with a figure-eight action.

4 Spoon the mixture into a freezerproof container and place in the freezer for about 3 hours.

5 To serve, scoop the chocolate dessert into sundae glasses and drizzle with a little Marsala. Top with whipped cream and decorate with the reserved grated chocolate. Serve immediately.

tiramisù

ingredients

SERVES 4

7 fl oz/200 ml/scant 1 cup
    strong black coffee, cooled
    to room temperature
4 tbsp orange liqueur,
    such as Cointreau
3 tbsp orange juice
16 Italian ladyfingers
9 oz/250 g/1^1/8 cups
    Mascarpone cheese
10 fl oz/300 ml/1^1/4 cups
    heavy cream,
    lightly whipped
3 tbsp confectioners' sugar
grated rind of 1 orange
2^1/4 oz/60 g semisweet
    chocolate, grated

to decorate

chopped toasted almonds
crystallized orange peel
chocolate shavings

method

1 Pour the cooled coffee into a pitcher and stir in the orange liqueur and orange juice. Place 8 of the ladyfingers in the bottom of a serving dish, then pour over half of the coffee mixture.

2 Place the Mascarpone in a separate bowl together with the cream, confectioners' sugar, and orange rind and mix well. Spread half of the Mascarpone mixture over the coffee-soaked ladyfingers, then arrange the remaining ladyfingers on top. Pour over the remaining coffee mixture then spread over the remaining Mascarpone mixture. Sprinkle over the grated chocolate and let chill in the refrigerator for at least 2 hours.

3 Serve decorated with the chopped toasted almonds, crystallized orange peel, and chocolate shavings.

cherry tiramisù

ingredients

SERVES 4

7 fl oz/200 ml/generous
  3/4 cup strong black
  coffee, cooled to room
  temperature
6 tbsp cherry brandy
16 trifle sponges
9 oz/250 g/1 1/4 cups
  Mascarpone
10 fl oz/300 ml/1 1/4 cups
  heavy cream,
  lightly whipped
3 tbsp confectioner's sugar
9 1/2 oz/275 g sweet cherries,
  halved and pitted
2 1/4 oz/60 g chocolate,
  curls or grated
whole cherries, to decorate

method

1 Pour the cooled coffee into a pitcher and stir in the cherry brandy. Put half of the trifle sponges into the bottom of a serving dish, then pour over half of the coffee mixture.

2 Put the Mascarpone into a separate bowl along with the cream and sugar, and mix together well. Spread half of the Mascarpone mixture over the coffee-soaked trifle sponges, then top with half of the cherries. Arrange the remaining trifle sponges on top. Pour over the remaining coffee mixture and top with the remaining cherries. Finish with a layer of Mascarpone mixture. Scatter over the grated chocolate, cover with plastic wrap, and chill in the refrigerator for at least 2 hours.

3 Remove from the refrigerator, decorate with cherries, and serve.

cassata

ingredients

SERVES 6–8

4 oz/115 g/generous $^1/_2$ cup granulated sugar

5 fl oz/150 ml/$^2/_3$ cup water

2 egg whites

2 oz/55 g/scant $^1/_3$ cup chopped blanched almonds

2 oz/55 g/scant $^1/_3$ cup mixed dried fruit

2 oz/55 g/scant $^1/_3$ cup candied cherries, chopped

10 fl oz/300 ml/1$^1/_4$ cups heavy whipping cream

method

1 Line a 2-lb/900-g loaf pan or 48-fl oz/1.5 liter/6-cup oblong freezerproof plastic container with parchment paper, allowing it to hang over the edges of the container so that the ice cream can be easily removed. Put the sugar and water in a small heavy-bottom pan and heat gently, stirring, until the sugar has dissolved. Bring to a boil, then boil, without stirring, for 5 minutes, or until a syrup has formed. Do not let it brown.

2 Meanwhile, whisk the egg whites until stiff and dry. Drizzle the hot syrup in a thin stream onto the whisked egg whites, whisking all the time until the mixture is thick, creamy, and fluffy. Continue whisking until the mixture is cold.

3 Add the nuts, dried fruit, and cherries to the meringue mixture and fold in until well blended. Whip the cream until it holds its shape, then fold in until well blended. Pour the mixture into the prepared pan or plastic container, cover, and freeze for 5 hours, or until firm or required.

4 To serve the ice cream, uncover, stand the pan or plastic container in hot water for a few seconds to loosen it, then invert it onto a serving dish. Remove the parchment paper and, using a hot knife, cut into slices.

chocolate brandy torte

ingredients

SERVES 12

base

3¹/₂ oz/100 g butter, plus extra
   for greasing
9 oz/250 g gingersnaps
2³/₄ oz/75 g semisweet
   chocolate

filling

8 oz/225 g semisweet chocolate
9 oz/250 g/generous 1 cup
   Mascarpone cheese
2 eggs, separated
3 tbsp brandy
10 fl oz/300 ml/1¹/₄ cups
   heavy cream
4 tbsp superfine sugar

to decorate

3¹/₂ fl oz/100 ml/generous
   ¹/₃ cup heavy cream
chocolate-covered coffee beans
unsweetened cocoa powder, to
   serve

method

1 Grease the bottom and sides of a 9-inch/
23-cm springform cake pan. Place the
gingersnaps in a plastic bag and crush with
a rolling pin. Transfer to a bowl. Place the
chocolate and butter in a small pan and
heat gently until melted, then pour over the
cookies. Mix well, then press into the prepared
pan. Let chill while preparing the filling.

2 To make the filling, place the chocolate in a
heatproof bowl set over a pan of simmering
water, and heat, stirring, until melted. Remove
from the heat and beat in the Mascarpone
cheese, egg yolks, and brandy.

3 Whip the cream until just holding its shape.
Fold in the chocolate mixture.

4 Whisk the egg whites in a spotlessly clean,
greasefree bowl until soft peaks form. Add the
sugar, a little at a time, and whisk until thick
and glossy. Fold into the chocolate mixture,
in 2 batches, until just mixed.

5 Spoon the mixture into the prepared base
and let chill in the refrigerator for at least
2 hours. Carefully transfer to a serving plate.
To decorate, whip the cream and pipe onto
the cheesecake, add the chocolate-covered
coffee beans, dust with unsweetened cocoa
powder, and serve.

new york cheesecake

ingredients

SERVES 8–10

6 tbsp butter

7 oz/200 g graham crackers, crushed

sunflower oil, for brushing

14 oz/400 g/1^3/$_4$ cups cream cheese

2 large eggs

5 oz/140 g/^{3}/$_4$ cup superfine sugar

1^1/$_2$ tsp vanilla extract

16 fl oz/450 ml/2 cups sour cream

blueberry topping

2 oz/55 g/generous ^{1}/$_4$ cup superfine sugar

4 tbsp water

9 oz/250 g/1^5/$_8$ cups fresh blueberries

1 tsp arrowroot

method

1 Melt the butter in a pan over low heat. Stir in the crackers, then spread in an 8-inch/20-cm springform pan brushed with oil. Place the cream cheese, eggs, ^{2}/$_3$ of the sugar, and ^{1}/$_2$ teaspoon of the vanilla extract in a food processor. Process until smooth. Pour over the cracker base and smooth the top. Place on a baking sheet and bake in a preheated oven, 375°F/190°C, for 20 minutes until set. Remove from the oven and leave for 20 minutes. Leave the oven switched on.

2 Mix the cream with the remaining sugar and vanilla extract in a bowl. Spoon over the cheesecake. Return it to the oven for 10 minutes, let cool, then chill in the refrigerator for 8 hours, or overnight.

3 To make the topping, place the sugar in a pan with 2 tablespoons of the water over low heat and stir until the sugar has dissolved. Increase the heat, add the blueberries, cover, and cook for a few minutes, or until they begin to soften. Remove from the heat. Mix the arrowroot and remaining water in a bowl, add to the fruit, and stir until smooth. Return to low heat. Cook until the juice thickens and turns translucent. Let cool.

4 Remove the cheesecake from the pan 1 hour before serving. Spoon the fruit topping over and let chill until ready to serve.

irish cream cheesecake

ingredients

SERVES 12

oil, for brushing

6 oz/175 g chocolate chip
    cookies

2 oz/55 g butter

filling

8 oz/225 g semisweet
    chocolate

8 oz/225 g milk chocolate

2 oz/55 g/³/₄ cup golden
    superfine sugar

12 oz/350 g/1¹/₂ cups
    cream cheese

15 fl oz/425 ml/1³/₄ cups
    heavy cream, whipped

3 tbsp Irish cream liqueur

crème fraîche or sour cream,
    to serve

fresh fruit, to serve

method

1 Line the base of a 20-cm/8-inch springform tin with foil and brush the sides with oil. Place the cookies in a polythene bag and crush with a rolling pin. Place the butter in a pan and heat gently until just melted, then stir in the crushed biscuits. Press the mixture into the base of the tin and chill in the refrigerator for 1 hour.

2 To make the filling, melt the semisweet and milk chocolate together, stir to combine and leave to cool. Place the sugar and cream cheese in a large bowl and beat together until smooth, then fold in the whipped cream. Fold the mixture gently into the melted chocolate, then stir in the Irish cream liqueur.

3 Spoon the filling over the chilled biscuit base and smooth the surface. Cover and leave to chill in the refrigerator for 2 hours, or until quite firm. Transfer to a serving plate and cut into small slices. Serve with a spoonful of crème fraîche and fresh fruit.

ice creams
& sherbets

Ice creams and sherbets are so special that you might be forgiven for thinking there is some magic and mystery to their creation! In fact, they are surprisingly easy to make.

When making ice creams and sherbets, it is useful, but by no means essential, to have an ice-cream maker. You simply prepare the mixture and pop it into the machine, following the manufacturer's instructions and keeping an eye on the recipe in case you need to add extra ingredients during the freezing process. Don't worry, however, if you don't have an ice-cream maker—you can simply transfer the prepared mixture into a shallow freezerproof container and freeze for 2 hours, or until it is beginning to freeze around the edges. At this point, beat it well with a fork, then return it to the freezer until frozen. Transfer it from the freezer to the refrigerator about 30 minutes before you plan to serve it, to soften a little.

Armed with the tools for making a frozen dessert, the choice is now yours! There are one or two very simple recipes here—Banana and Coconut Ice Cream and Marshmallow Ice Cream take only moments to prepare and are easy to freeze—but it's worth mastering the art of making a simple sherbet and a vanilla custard ice cream, because once you've done that, the list of variations is almost endless!

cappuccino ice cream

ingredients

SERVES 4

5 fl oz/150 ml/²/₃ cup
   whole milk
20 fl oz/600 ml/2¹/₂ cups
   heavy whipping cream
4 tbsp finely ground
   fresh coffee
3 large egg yolks
3¹/₂ oz/100 g/generous
   ¹/₂ cup superfine sugar
unsweetened cocoa,
   for dusting
chocolate-coated coffee beans,
   to decorate

method

1 Pour the milk and 16 fl oz/500 ml/2 cups of the cream into a heavy-bottom pan, stir in the coffee, and bring almost to a boil. Remove from the heat, let infuse for 5 minutes, then strain through a paper filter or a strainer lined with cheesecloth.

2 Put the egg yolks and sugar in a large bowl and whisk together until pale and the mixture leaves a trail when the whisk is lifted. Slowly add the milk mixture, stirring all the time with a wooden spoon. Strain the mixture into the rinsed-out pan or a double boiler and cook over low heat for 10–15 minutes, stirring all the time, until the mixture thickens enough to coat the back of the spoon. Do not let the mixture boil or it will curdle. Remove the custard from the heat and let cool for at least 1 hour, stirring from time to time to prevent a skin forming.

3 Churn the cold custard in an ice-cream maker following the manufacturer's instructions.

4 To serve, whip the remaining cream until it holds its shape. Scoop the ice cream into wide-brimmed coffee cups and smooth the tops. Spoon the whipped cream over the top of each and sprinkle with unsweetened cocoa. Decorate with chocolate-coated coffee beans.

rich vanilla ice cream

ingredients

SERVES 4–6

10 fl oz/300 ml/1^1/4 cups light
  cream and 10 fl oz/300
  ml/1^1/4 cups heavy cream
  or 20 fl oz/600 ml/2^1/2
  cups heavy whipping
  cream

1 vanilla bean

4 large egg yolks

3^1/2 oz/100 g/generous
  ^{1}/2 cup superfine sugar

method

1 Pour the light and heavy cream or heavy whipping cream into a large heavy-bottom pan. Split open the vanilla bean and scrape out the seeds into the cream, then add the whole vanilla bean too. Bring almost to a boil, then remove from the heat and let infuse for 30 minutes.

2 Put the egg yolks and sugar in a large bowl and whisk together until pale and the mixture leaves a trail when the whisk is lifted. Remove the vanilla bean from the cream, then slowly add the cream to the egg mixture, stirring all the time with a wooden spoon. Strain the mixture into the rinsed-out pan or a double boiler and cook over low heat for 10–15 minutes, stirring all the time, until the mixture thickens enough to coat the back of the spoon. Do not let the mixture boil or it will curdle. Remove the custard from the heat and let cool for at least 1 hour, stirring from time to time to prevent a skin forming.

3 Churn the custard in an ice-cream maker following the manufacturer's instructions. Serve immediately if wished, or transfer to a freezerproof container, cover with a lid, and store in the freezer.

dairy strawberry ice cream

ingredients

SERVES 6

8 oz/225 g/generous 1 cup
   superfine sugar

5 fl oz/150 ml/^{2}/$_3$ cup water

2 lb/900 g fresh strawberries,
   plus extra to decorate

juice of ^{1}/$_2$ lemon

juice of ^{1}/$_2$ orange

10 fl oz/300 ml/1^1/$_4$ cups
   heavy whipping cream

method

1 Put the sugar and water in a heavy-bottom pan and heat gently, stirring, until the sugar has dissolved. Bring to a boil, then, without stirring, boil for 5 minutes to form a syrup. Toward the end of the cooking time, keep an eye on the mixture to ensure that it does not burn. Immediately remove the syrup from the heat and let cool for at least 1 hour.

2 Meanwhile, push the strawberries through a nylon strainer into a bowl to form a purée. When the syrup is cold, add the strawberry purée to it with the lemon juice and orange juice and stir well together. Whip the cream until it holds its shape. Keep in the refrigerator until ready to use.

3 If using an ice-cream maker, fold the strawberry mixture into the whipped cream, then churn in the machine following the manufacturer's instructions. Alternatively, freeze the mixture in a freezerproof container, uncovered, for 1–2 hours, or until it starts to set around the edges. Turn the mixture into a bowl and stir with a fork or beat in a food processor until smooth. Fold in the whipped cream. Return to the freezer and freeze for an additional 2–3 hours, or until firm or required. Cover the container with a lid for storing. Serve decorated with strawberries.

rippled black currant ice cream

ingredients

SERVES 6–8

15 fl oz/450 ml/scant
    2 cups whole milk

1 vanilla bean

9 oz/250 g/generous
    $1^1/_4$ cups superfine sugar

4 egg yolks

8 oz/225 g/scant 2 cups fresh
    black currants, stripped
    from their stalks, plus
    extra to decorate

6 tbsp water

15 fl oz/450 ml/scant 2 cups
    heavy whipping cream

method

1 Pour the milk into a pan, add the vanilla bean, and bring almost to a boil. Let infuse for 30 minutes, then remove the vanilla bean.

2 Put 4 oz/115 g/scant $^2/_3$ cup of the sugar and the egg yolks in a large bowl and whisk until pale and the mixture leaves a trail when the whisk is lifted. Slowly add the milk, stirring constantly with a wooden spoon. Strain the mixture into a clean pan and cook over low heat for 10–15 minutes, stirring, until the mixture coats the back of the spoon. Do not let boil. Remove from the heat and let cool for at least 1 hour, stirring occasionally.

3 Put the black currants in a heavy-bottom pan with the remaining sugar and the water. Heat gently, stirring, to dissolve the sugar, then let simmer gently for 10 minutes, or until the black currants are very soft. Push through a nylon strainer into a bowl to remove the seeds, then let the purée cool.

4 Whip the cream until it holds its shape. Fold the custard into the cream, then churn in an ice-cream maker. Just before the ice cream freezes, spread half in a freezerproof container. Pour over half the black currant purée, then repeat the layers. Freeze for 1–2 hours, or until firm. Serve decorated with black currants.

lemon yogurt ice cream

ingredients

SERVES 4–6

2–3 lemons

20 fl oz/600 ml/scant 2$^1/_2$-cup
   carton strained
   plain yogurt

5 fl oz/150 ml/$^2/_3$ cup
   heavy cream

3$^1/_2$ oz/100 g/$^1/_2$ cup
   superfine sugar

finely pared orange rind,
   to decorate

method

1 Squeeze the juice from the lemons—you need 6 tablespoons in total. Put the juice into a bowl, add the yogurt, cream, and sugar, and mix well together.

2 If using an ice-cream maker, churn the mixture in the machine following the manufacturer's instructions. Alternatively, freeze the mixture in a freezerproof container, uncovered, for 1–2 hours, or until it starts to set around the edges. Turn the mixture into a bowl and stir with a fork or beat in a food processor until smooth. Return to the freezer and freeze for an additional 2–3 hours, or until firm or required. Cover the container with a lid for storing. Serve with finely pared orange rind.

blood orange ice cream

ingredients

SERVES 4–6

3 large blood oranges, washed

3 fl oz/85 ml/$1/3$ cup lowfat
    milk

3 fl oz/85 ml/$1/3$ cup
    light cream

$41/2$ oz/125 g/scant $3/4$ cup
    superfine sugar

4 large egg yolks

16 fl oz/450 ml/2 cups
    heavy cream

$1/8$ tsp vanilla extract

shortbread cookies, to serve

method

1 Thinly pare the rind from 2 of the oranges, reserving a few strips for decoration, and finely grate the rind from the third. Squeeze the oranges to give 4 fl oz/125 ml/$1/2$ cup juice and set aside.

2 Pour the milk and cream into a pan with the pared orange rind. Bring to a boil, then remove from the heat; set aside to infuse for at least 30 minutes.

3 Put the sugar and egg yolks in a heatproof bowl that fits over the pan without touching the bottom and beat until thick and creamy.

4 Return the milk mixture to the heat and bring to a simmer. Pour the milk onto the eggs and whisk until well blended. Rinse the pan, put a small amount of water in it and, placing it over medium heat, bring the water to a simmer. Reduce the heat. Put the bowl on top and stir for about 20 minutes until a thick custard forms that coats the back of the spoon; the water must not touch the bottom of the bowl or the eggs might scramble.

5 Strain the mixture into a clean bowl. Stir in the finely grated orange rind and set aside for 10 minutes. Stir in the reserved juice, heavy cream, and vanilla extract. Transfer to an ice-cream maker and freeze following the manufacturer's instructions. Decorate with strips of the reserved rind and serve with shortbread cookies.

banana ice cream

ingredients

SERVES 8

3 bananas

2 tbsp lemon juice

1 tbsp white rum (optional)

7 oz/200 g/1 cup
    confectioners' sugar

20 fl oz/600 ml/2$\frac{1}{2}$ cups
    heavy whipping cream

method

1 Peel and slice the bananas, then put the flesh in a food processor or blender. Add the lemon juice and process to form a very smooth purée. Turn the mixture into a large bowl. Alternatively, sprinkle the lemon juice over the banana slices, then push the flesh through a nylon strainer to form a purée. Add the rum, if using, and mix well together.

2 Sift the confectioners' sugar into the mixture and beat until well mixed. Whip the cream until it holds its shape. Keep in the refrigerator until ready to use.

3 If using an ice-cream maker, fold the whipped cream into the banana mixture, then churn the mixture in the machine following the manufacturer's instructions. Alternatively, freeze the mixture in a freezerproof container, uncovered, for 1–2 hours, or until it starts to set around the edges. Turn the mixture into a bowl and stir with a fork or beat in a food processor until smooth. Fold in the whipped cream. Return to the freezer and freeze for an additional 2–3 hours, or until firm or required. Cover the container with a lid for storing.

banana & coconut ice cream

ingredients

SERVES 6–8

3 oz/85 g block creamed
   coconut, chopped
20 fl oz/600 ml/2$^{1}/_{2}$ cups
   heavy cream
8 oz/225 g/$^{1}/_{2}$ cup
   confectioners' sugar
2 bananas
1 tsp lemon juice
fresh fruit, to serve (optional)

method

1 Put the creamed coconut in a small bowl. Add just enough boiling water to cover and stir until dissolved. Let cool.

2 Whip the cream with the sugar until thick but still floppy. Mash the bananas with the lemon juice and whisk gently into the cream, along with the cold coconut.

3 Transfer to a freezerproof container and freeze overnight. Serve in scoops with fresh fruit (optional).

pistachio ice cream

ingredients

SERVES 4

20 fl oz/300 ml/1¼ cups
    heavy cream
5½ oz/150 g/⅔ cup
    strained yogurt
2 tbsp milk
3 tbsp honey
green food coloring
1¾ oz/50 g/⅔ cup shelled
    unsalted pistachio nuts,
    finely chopped

pistachio praline

oil, for brushing
5½ oz/150 g/¾ cup
    granulated sugar
3 tbsp water
1¾ oz/50 g/⅔ cup shelled,
    whole, unsalted
    pistachio nuts

method

1 Set the freezer to its lowest setting. Put the cream, yogurt, milk, and honey in a bowl and mix together. Add a few drops of green food coloring to tint the mixture pale green and stir in well. Pour the mixture into a shallow freezer container and freeze, uncovered, for 1–2 hours, until beginning to set around the edges. Turn the mixture into a bowl and, with a fork, stir until smooth then stir in the pistachio nuts. Return to the freezer container, cover, and freeze for another 2–3 hours, until firm. Alternatively, use an ice-cream maker, following the manufacturer's instructions.

2 To make the pistachio praline, brush a baking sheet with oil. Put the sugar and water in a pan and heat gently, stirring, until the sugar has dissolved, then allow to bubble gently, without stirring, for 6–10 minutes, until lightly golden brown.

3 Remove the pan from the heat and stir in the pistachio nuts. Immediately pour the mixture onto the baking sheet and spread out evenly. Let it stand in a cool place for about 1 hour, until cold and hardened, then crush it in a plastic bag with a hammer.

4 About 30 minutes before serving, remove the ice cream from the freezer and let stand at room temperature to soften slightly. To serve, scatter the praline over the ice cream.

cinnamon ice cream

ingredients

SERVES 4–6

10 fl oz/300 ml/1¹/₄ cups
    heavy whipping cream
1 tsp ground cinnamon
20-fl oz/600-ml/scant 2¹/₂-
    cup carton fresh custard
1 tbsp lemon juice
3¹/₂ oz/100 g/scant ¹/₂ cup
    confectioners' sugar

method

1 Pour the cream into a heavy-bottom pan, add the cinnamon and stir together. Bring almost to a boil, then remove from the heat and let infuse for 30 minutes.

2 Put the custard and lemon juice in a large bowl. Sift in the confectioners' sugar, then stir together. Pour in the cinnamon cream and whisk together until mixed.

3 If using an ice-cream maker, churn the mixture in the machine following the manufacturer's instructions. Alternatively, freeze the mixture in a freezerproof container, uncovered, for 1–2 hours, or until it starts to set around the edges.

4 Turn the mixture into a bowl and stir with a fork or beat in a food processor until smooth. Return to the freezer and freeze for an additional 2–3 hours, or until firm or required. Cover the container with a lid for storing.

maple syrup & walnut ice cream

ingredients

SERVES 6

4 oz/115 g/scant 1 cup
   walnut pieces
5 fl oz/150 ml/²/₃ cup
   maple syrup
10 fl oz/300 ml/1¹/₄ cups
   heavy cream
7 fl oz/200 ml canned
   evaporated milk, well chilled

method

1 Process the walnut pieces in a food processor until finely chopped but be careful not to process them into a purée. Set aside.

2 Mix the syrup and cream together until well blended. Pour the chilled evaporated milk into a large bowl and whisk until thick and doubled in volume. The mixture should leave a trail when the whisk is lifted. Add the syrup mixture to the whisked milk and fold together.

3 If using an ice-cream maker, churn the mixture in the machine following the manufacturer's instructions. Just before the ice cream freezes, add the chopped nuts. Alternatively, freeze the mixture in a freezerproof container, uncovered, for 1–2 hours, or until it starts to set around the edges. Turn the mixture into a bowl and stir with a fork or beat in a food processor until smooth. Stir in the chopped nuts, then return to the freezer and freeze for an additional 2–3 hours, or until firm or required. Cover the container with a lid for storing.

dark chocolate ice cream

ingredients

SERVES 6

2 eggs

2 egg yolks

4 oz/115 g/generous ½ cup golden superfine sugar

10 fl oz/300 ml/1¼ cups light cream

8 oz/225 g semisweet chocolate, chopped

10 fl oz/300 ml/1¼ cups heavy cream

4 tbsp brandy

method

1 Place the whole eggs, egg yolks, and sugar in a heatproof bowl and beat together until well blended. Place the light cream and chocolate in a pan and heat gently until the chocolate has melted, then continue to heat, stirring constantly, until almost boiling. Pour onto the egg mixture, stirring vigorously, then set the bowl over a pan of gently simmering water, making sure that the base of the bowl does not touch the water.

2 Cook, stirring constantly, until the mixture lightly coats the back of the spoon. Strain into a separate bowl and let cool. Place the heavy cream and brandy in a separate bowl and whip until slightly thickened, then fold into the cooled chocolate mixture.

3 Freeze in an ice-cream maker, following the manufacturer's instructions. Alternatively, pour the mixture into a large freezerproof container, then cover and freeze for 2 hours, or until just frozen. Spoon into a bowl and beat with a fork to break down the ice crystals. Return to the freezer for 2 hours, or until firm. Transfer the ice cream to the refrigerator 30 minutes before serving. Scoop the ice cream into 4 serving dishes or coffee cups and serve.

chocolate & honey ice cream

ingredients

SERVES 6

18 fl oz/500 ml/2 cups milk

7 oz/200 g semisweet
   chocolate, broken
   into pieces

4 eggs, separated

3 oz/85 g/scant $^1/_2$ cup
   superfine sugar

pinch of salt

2 tbsp honey

12 fresh strawberries,
   washed and hulled

sprig of fresh mint, to garnish

method

1 Pour the milk into a pan, add $5^1/_2$ oz/150 g of the chocolate, and stir over medium heat for 3–5 minutes, until melted. Remove the pan from the heat and set aside.

2 Beat the egg yolks with all but 1 tablespoon of the sugar in a separate bowl until pale and thickened. Gradually beat in the milk mixture, a little at a time. Return the mixture to a clean pan and cook over low heat, whisking constantly, until smooth and thickened. Remove from the heat and let cool. Cover with plastic wrap and chill in the refrigerator for 30 minutes.

3 Whisk the egg whites with a pinch of salt until soft peaks form. Gradually whisk in the remaining sugar and whisk until stiff and glossy. Stir the honey into the chocolate mixture, then gently fold in the egg whites. Divide among 6 individual freezerproof molds and freeze for at least 4 hours.

4 Meanwhile, melt the remaining chocolate until smooth in a heatproof bowl set over a pan of barely simmering water. Half-coat the strawberries in the melted chocolate. Place on a sheet of baking parchment to set. Transfer the ice cream to the refrigerator for 10 minutes before serving. Serve decorated with the chocolate-coated strawberries, and garnish with a sprig of fresh mint.

marshmallow ice cream

ingredients

SERVES 4

3 oz/85 g semisweet
    chocolate, broken
    into pieces
6 oz/175 g white marshmallows
5 fl oz/150 ml/²/₃ cup milk
10 fl oz/300 ml/1¹/₄ cups
    heavy cream
fresh fruit, to serve

method

1 Put the semisweet chocolate and marsh-mallows in a pan and pour in the milk. Warm over very low heat until the chocolate and marshmallows have melted. Remove from the heat and let cool completely.

2 Whip the cream until thick, then fold it into the cold chocolate mixture with a metal spoon. Pour into a 1-lb/450-g loaf pan and freeze for at least 2 hours, until firm (it will keep for 1 month in the freezer). Serve the ice cream with fresh fruit.

mango sherbet

ingredients

SERVES 4–6

2 large ripe mangoes

juice of 1 lemon

pinch of salt

3$^{1}/_{2}$ oz/100 g/generous
   $^{1}/_{2}$ cup sugar

3 tbsp water

method

1 Thinly peel the mangoes, holding them over a bowl to catch the juices. Cut the flesh away from the central pit and put in a food processor or blender. Add the mango juice, lemon juice, and salt and process to form a smooth purée. Push the mango purée through a nylon strainer into the bowl.

2 Put the sugar and water in a heavy-bottom pan and heat gently, stirring, until the sugar has dissolved. Bring to a boil, without stirring, then remove from the heat and let cool slightly.

3 Pour the syrup into the mango purée and mix well together. Let cool, then chill the mango syrup in the refrigerator for 2 hours, or until cold.

4 If using an ice-cream maker, churn the mixture in the machine following the manufacturer's instructions. Alternatively, freeze the mixture in a freezerproof container, uncovered, for 3–4 hours, or until mushy. Turn the mixture into a bowl and stir with a fork or beat in a food processor to break down the ice crystals. Return to the freezer and freeze for an additional 3–4 hours, or until firm or required. Cover the container with a lid for storing.

pineapple & lime sherbet

ingredients

SERVES 4

8 oz/225 g/generous 1 cup
   superfine sugar
20 fl oz/600 ml/2^1/$_2$ cups
   water
grated rind and juice of 2 limes
1 small pineapple, peeled,
   quartered, and chopped

method

1 Put the sugar and water into a pan and heat gently, stirring until the sugar has dissolved. Bring to a boil and let simmer for 10 minutes.

2 Stir in the grated rind and half the lime juice. Remove from the heat and let cool.

3 Put the pineapple in a blender or food processor and process until smooth. Add to the cold syrup with the remaining lime juice. Pour into a freezerproof container and freeze until crystals have formed around the edge.

4 Turn out the sherbet into a bowl. Beat well with a fork to break up the crystals. Return to the freezer and chill overnight. Serve in scoops.

gooseberry & elderberry flower sherbet

ingredients

SERVES 6

3¹/₂ oz/100 g/generous ¹/₂ cup sugar

20 fl oz/600 ml/2¹/₂ cups water

1 lb 2 oz/500 g fresh gooseberries

4 fl oz/125 ml/¹/₂ cup elderberry flower cordial

1 tbsp lemon juice

few drops of green food coloring (optional)

4 fl oz/125 ml/¹/₂ cup heavy cream

method

1 Put the sugar and water in a heavy-bottom pan and heat gently, stirring, until the sugar has dissolved. Bring to a boil, then add the gooseberries, without trimming them, and let simmer, stirring occasionally, for 10 minutes, or until very tender. Let cool for 5 minutes.

2 Put the gooseberries in a food processor or blender and process to form a smooth purée. Push the purée through a nylon strainer into a bowl to remove the seeds. Let cool for at least 1 hour.

3 Add the elderberry flower cordial and lemon juice to the cold gooseberry purée and stir together until well mixed. If wished, add the food coloring to tint the mixture pale green. Stir the cream into the mixture.

4 If using an ice-cream maker, churn the mixture in the machine following the manufacturer's instructions. Alternatively, freeze the mixture in a freezerproof container, uncovered, for 3–4 hours, or until mushy. Turn the mixture into a bowl and stir with a fork or beat in a food processor to break down the ice crystals. Return to the freezer and freeze for an additional 3–4 hours, or until firm or required. Cover the container with a lid for storing.

red berry sherbet

ingredients

SERVES 6

6 oz/140 g/1¹/₄ cups red
   currants, plus extra
   to decorate
6 oz/140 g/1¹/₄ cups
   raspberries, plus extra
   to decorate
6 fl oz/175 m/³/₄ cup water
3¹/₂ oz/100 g/generous
   ¹/₂ cup sugar
5 fl oz/150 ml/²/₃ cup
   cranberry juice
2 egg whites

method

1 Strip the red currants from their stalks using the tines of a fork and put them in a large heavy-bottom pan together with the raspberries. Add 2 tablespoons of the water and cook over medium heat for 10 minutes, or until soft. Push the fruit through a nylon strainer into a bowl to form a purée.

2 Put the sugar and the remaining water into the rinsed-out pan and heat gently, stirring, until the sugar has dissolved. Bring to a boil, then boil, without stirring, for 10 minutes to form a syrup. Do not let it brown. Remove from the heat and let cool for at least 1 hour. When cold, stir the fruit purée and cranberry juice into the syrup.

3 If using an ice-cream maker, churn the mixture in the machine following the manufacturer's instructions. When the mixture starts to freeze, whisk the egg whites until they just hold their shape but are not dry, then add to the mixture and continue churning. Serve sprinkled with extra fruits.

berry yogurt ice

ingredients

SERVES 4

4^1/$_2$ oz/125 g/1^1/$_8$ cups raspberries

4^1/$_2$ oz/125 g/^{3}/$_4$ cup blackberries

4^1/$_2$ oz/125 g/^{3}/$_4$ cup strawberries

1 large egg, separated

6 fl oz/175 ml/^{3}/$_4$ cup strained plain yogurt

4 fl oz/125 ml/^{1}/$_2$ cup red wine

2^1/$_4$ tsp powdered gelatin

fresh berries, to decorate

method

1 Place the raspberries, blackberries, and strawberries in a blender or food processor and process until a smooth purée forms. Rub the purée through a strainer into a bowl to remove the seeds.

2 Stir the egg yolk and yogurt into the berry purée.

3 Pour the wine into a heatproof bowl set over a pan of water. Sprinkle the gelatin on the surface of the wine and let stand for 5 minutes to soften. Heat the pan of water and simmer until the gelatin has dissolved. Pour the mixture into the berry purée in a steady stream, whisking constantly. Transfer the mixture to a freezerproof container and freeze for 2 hours, or until slushy.

4 Whisk the egg white in a spotlessly clean, grease-free bowl until very stiff. Remove the berry mixture from the freezer and fold in the egg white. Return to the freezer and freeze for 2 hours, or until firm.

5 To serve, scoop the berry yogurt ice into glass dishes, and decorate with fresh berries of your choice.

lemon water ice

ingredients

SERVES 6

7 oz/200 g/scant 1 cup sugar

15 fl oz/450 ml/scant
2 cups water

6–9 large lemons

lemon slices, to decorate

method

1 Put the sugar and water in a heavy-bottom pan and heat gently, stirring, until the sugar has dissolved. Bring to a boil, then boil, without stirring, for 10 minutes to form a syrup. Do not let it brown.

2 Meanwhile, using a potato peeler, thinly pare the rind from 4 of the lemons. Remove the syrup from the heat and add the pared lemon rind. Let cool for at least 1 hour.

3 Squeeze the juice from the lemons and strain into a measuring cup—you need 15 fl oz/450 ml/scant 2 cups in total. When the syrup is cold, strain it into a bowl, add the lemon juice, and stir together until well mixed.

4 If using an ice-cream maker, churn the mixture in the machine following the manufacturer's instructions. Alternatively, freeze the mixture in a freezerproof container, uncovered, for 3–4 hours, or until mushy. Turn the mixture into a bowl and stir with a fork or beat in a food processor to break down the ice crystals. Return to the freezer and freeze for an additional 3–4 hours, or until firm or required. Cover the container with a lid for storing. Serve decorated with lemon slices.

coffee granita

ingredients

SERVES 6

2 tbsp sugar

20 fl oz/600 ml/2^1/$_2$ cups
water

1^3/$_4$ oz/50 g fresh Italian
coffee, finely ground

4 fl oz/125 ml/^{1}/$_2$ cup
heavy whipping cream,
whipped, to serve

method

1 Put the sugar and water in a heavy-bottom pan and heat gently, stirring, until the sugar has dissolved. Bring to a boil, then remove from the heat and stir in the coffee. Let stand for 1 hour to allow the mixture to infuse and cool completely.

2 Strain the coffee through a paper filter or a strainer lined with cheesecloth. Pour the coffee into 2 shallow freezerproof containers and freeze, uncovered, for 30 minutes.

3 Turn both mixtures into a bowl and stir with a fork, or beat in a food processor, to break down the ice crystals. Return to the freezer and freeze, repeating the breaking down of the ice crystals about every 30 minutes until the granita is granular. This process will take 3–4 hours in total. Cover the container with a lid for storing.

4 Serve the granita in glasses, straight from the freezer, broken into tiny ice crystals. Top each glass with a little whipped cream.

chocolate sherbet

ingredients

SERVES 6

2 oz/55 g/^{1}/$_2$ cup
unsweetened cocoa

5^1/$_2$ oz/150 g/generous
^{3}/$_4$ cup golden
superfine sugar

2 tsp instant coffee powder

2 cups water

crisp cookies, to serve

method

1 Sift the unsweetened cocoa into a small, heavy-bottom pan and add the superfine sugar, coffee powder, and a little of the water. Using a wooden spoon, mix together to form a thin paste, then gradually stir in the remaining water. Bring the mixture to a boil over low heat and let simmer gently for 8 minutes, stirring frequently.

2 Remove the pan from the heat and let cool. Transfer the mixture to a bowl, cover with plastic wrap and place in the refrigerator until well chilled. Freeze in an ice-cream maker, following the manufacturer's instructions. Alternatively, pour the mixture into a large freezerproof container, then cover and freeze for 2 hours. Remove the sherbet from the freezer and beat to break down the ice crystals. Freeze for an additional 6 hours, beating the sherbet every 2 hours.

3 Transfer the sherbet to the refrigerator 30 minutes before serving. Scoop into 6 small bowls and serve with crisp cookies.